New England
DESSERTS

Classic and Creative Recipes for All Seasons

Tammy Donroe Inman

Globe
Pequot

Essex, Connecticut

For Rich

In memory of Amy and Jocelyn Gannon

Globe
Pequot

An imprint of Globe Pequot, the trade division of
The Rowman & Littlefield Publishing Group, Inc.
4501 Forbes Blvd., Ste. 200
Lanham, MD 20706
www.rowman.com

Distributed by NATIONAL BOOK NETWORK

Photography by Tammy Donroe Inman with additional photos from GomezDavid/
E+ via Getty Images (page 49); Baber Photography/iStock/Getty Images Plus via
Getty Images (pages 86–87); Adél Békefi/Moment via Getty Images (pages 142–143);
mtv2020/iStock/Getty Images Plus via Getty Images (page 158); AnnaPustynnikova
via iStock/Getty Images Plus (pages 186–187)

British Library Cataloguing in Publication Information available

Library of Congress Cataloging-in-Publication Data available

978-1-4930-6374-1 (cloth : alk. paper)
978-1-4930-6375-8 (electronic)

∞™ The paper used in this publication meets the minimum requirements of American National Standard for Information Sciences—Permanence of Paper for Printed
Library Materials, ANSI/NISO Z39.48-1992.

Contents

Introduction

New England is a special place. Nowhere else in the country can you witness the seasons unfold in such spectacular fashion. Spring transforms the barren land into a verdant paradise, marking the transition with a flurry of apple and cherry blossoms, petals falling like pink and white confetti. Summer's sun-drenched fields and dappled orchards are flush with berries and stone fruits by July. Autumn's festive apple-picking and pumpkin-carving culminates in a dazzling finale of fiery orange, deep crimson, and burnished gold before the trees shed their festive frocks. And winter's sugar-dusted hills and sparkling ice sculptures glazed in the wake of the latest nor'easter have a stark beauty all their own. The ever-changing New England landscape is a feast for the senses.

One of the best ways to embrace these seasonal changes is through the local food, and desserts are my sweet spot. Each season has its own flavor. Spring rains coax up tart rhubarb for pies and crisps. It's not officially summer in New England until shortcake is soaked with juicy strawberries and cream. Soon black raspberries, blueberries, cherries, peaches, and plums make an appearance, begging for their own crisp toppings, buttery crusts, and melting pools of vanilla ice cream. With the arrival of fall come bushels of apples, pears, and pumpkins with a smattering of cranberries and a heady dose of mulling spices to help ease the transition to shorter days and cooler nights. And winter is all about deep, comforting flavors like butterscotch, caramel, chocolate, nuts, and dried fruits.

New England Desserts offers enticing recipes for fresh homemade cakes, cookies, candies, pies, crisps, cobblers, crumbles, and ice cream—for every season of the year. Think Rhubarb Ripple Ice Cream, Sweet Cherry Black Raspberry Cobbler, Caramel Apple Tarts, and Cranberry Walnut Steamed Pudding. All the classics are covered, from the traditional assembly of holiday pies (Apple, Pumpkin, Maple Walnut) to cookie plate favorites (Snickerdoodles, Joe Froggers, Snowballs) to kid-friendly comfort foods (Whoopie Pies, Butterscotch Pudding, Peppermint Stick Ice Cream). Regional specialties from each state are featured, including Maine Wild Blueberry Pie, Vermont Maple Walnut Fudge, Boston Cream Pie, and Rhode Island Coffee Milk Frappes. There are also plenty of new twists on old favorites, including inventive flavor combinations inspired by the different immigrant groups that have settled here over the generations: Peach Amaretti Ice Cream, Strawberry Rosewater Sorbet, and Honeydew Jalapeño Ice Pops.

This book gathers every New Englander's favorite dessert recipes into one place, giving each season its time in the sun. There's also a chapter for ice cream year round, including frappes and sundae toppings. What once was a summertime indulgence is now an evergreen favorite, as much at home in winter served alongside pies and crisps as it is in the heat of summer. Included are Connecticut Valley Vanilla, New Hampshire Strawberry, Beantown Chocolate, Rhode Island Coffee, Vermont Maple, and Maine Buttermilk and Sea Salt.

My New England Connection

I'm a New Englander, born and bred. I made my entrance into the world in southern Maine, a stone's throw from the rugged Atlantic coastline. My sandbox days passed under the shady pines of New Hampshire. In summer, I plucked strawberries from my mother's garden and grazed on wild blueberries in the woods. In winter, I tunneled through snowbanks like an Arctic mole. I spent my school years in the suburbs of Boston, Massachusetts, following the Freedom Trail, cheering on marathon runners, and attempting to learn how to bake from an old copy of Fannie Merritt Farmer's *The Boston Cooking-School Cook Book*. Summers slowly unspooled on the beaches of Cape Cod or with family in Connecticut, where ice cream was never far from my mind. I've lived in New England nearly my whole life—first by luck, later by choice.

I've always had a sweet tooth. The first words I learned how to read were "ice cream," and I kept my parents well informed of any ice cream–related signage from the back seat of the car. Growing up in a health-conscious household, I was constantly tormented by the seemingly endless assortment of sugary temptations that were off-limits: lushly frosted cakes, gooey chocolate chip cookies, satiny puddings, tantalizing blocks of fudge, and thickly bubbling fruit pies with ice cream melting all over the place. I felt a keen sense of deprivation. As an adult, I took matters into my own hands.

My quest to craft the perfect pie got off to a rocky start. But with practice and professional help from the Cambridge School of Culinary Arts, I gradually got a feel for working with pie dough, as well as other flaky pastries, molten sugar syrups, and fluffy meringues. My experience working for *Cook's Illustrated* and behind the scenes of the hit TV show *America's Test Kitchen* taught me how to test recipes rigorously (and brought me face-to-face with Julia Child!). On assignment for local magazines and newspapers, I had the opportunity to visits farms, restaurants, and festivals all over New England, informing my view that the best food is local food. After years as a cooking instructor for adults and children, I learned how to teach novice cooks how to bake without fear (and how to fix almost every mistake you can make). And the blog I wrote for 10 years (shout-out to my *Food on the Food* readers!) gave me the freedom to experiment in the kitchen and develop my own style—one rooted in tradition and buoyed, if not by Yankee ingenuity, then at least by the passionate whimsies of the blood-sugar-challenged.

New England Desserts celebrates my beloved New England and all the sweetness it has to offer, from the rocky fields and alpine mountains of Maine, Vermont, and New Hampshire, to the fertile river plains and coastal communities of Connecticut, Massachusetts, and Rhode Island. My hope is that you'll turn to this book again and again for the freshest seasonal desserts New England has to offer year-round. But, in truth, you don't need to live in New England to appreciate its seasonal flavors. It's the spirit and beauty of the region I'm trying to capture here. You can make these recipes pretty much anywhere, and most ingredients are easy to find. This book contains a mix of easy weekday recipes as well as more adventurous weekend projects and holiday-worthy desserts. Best of all, this cookbook offers recipes for every skill level, from beginner to expert, so anyone can enjoy the sweet rewards any time of year

What Is a New England Dessert?

Since the very first taste of maple syrup, New Englanders have pined for something sweet. Apple pie is perhaps the first dish that comes to mind when envisioning New England desserts (along with apple crisp, apple cake, apple tarts . . .). Apples are grown in every state in New England, and the arrival of fall is synonymous with apple-picking, hayrides, and apple cider doughnuts. Pumpkin pie is similarly universal in its appeal, with its festive association with Halloween and Thanksgiving. Blueberries feature prominently in Maine, where both native lowbush and cultivated highbush blueberries thrive in the region's acidic soil. Cranberries flourish in the boggy, glacier-gouged areas of southeastern Massachusetts and Cape Cod. Sugar maple trees, the best source for the region's famed maple syrup, grow all over New England, but especially in the northwest section of Vermont. And the region's dairy farming—not to mention the early ice industry—contributed to one of our most treasured local desserts: ice cream.

New England desserts embrace seasonal flavors and local ingredients. They tend toward unfussy, rustic preparations that rely on a frugal simplicity that showcases flavor. As I researched and developed recipes for this cookbook, I used the following principles as my guide:

Seasonality: First and foremost, the desserts in this book are inspired by the seasons. You don't make strawberry shortcake in the wintertime. I mean, you *can* (*Live Free or Die,* right, New Hampshire?), but it won't be as good without the sweetness of ripe, local strawberries. Cooking in season means you get the best-tasting ingredients at peak flavor, when they're most abundant, and also at their cheapest. That's why the recipes in this book are conveniently organized by season, so all the desserts you'll want to make *right now* are all together in one place.

Regionality: Many of the desserts in this book were invented or popularized in New England (like chocolate chip cookies and Thanksgiving-style pumpkin pie). Others have different or unknown origins but have become woven into the culinary fabric of the region over time. A New England dessert should be a recognizable part of the food culture in some way, and we should understand what that connection is. In a few cases, I've invented my own twist on a New England theme and only time will tell if it sticks.

Practicality: I tried to keep the recipes as simple as possible. I'm a lazy cook at heart, but I don't like to sacrifice flavor. I provide substitutions where appropriate, and I would encourage you to experiment based on what you have (but first consider whether you're willing to accept the consequences if your substitution doesn't work out exactly as planned).

Frugality: New Englanders are notoriously frugal, and I'm no exception. I try to keep cost in mind when developing recipes. However, some ingredients are inherently expensive. (I'm looking at you, maple syrup!) The good news is that your hard-earned cash will go straight back into the local economy, helping farmers continue growing the foods we love and be responsible stewards of this land.

Ingenuity: For some of the recipes in this book, I haven't strayed too far from tradition. For others, I've added a twist or two, updating or swapping out flavors and drawing inspiration from our diverse New England communities and the world around us. Still, the spirit of New England should remain.

Many dessert traditions are shared across state boundaries. Others, like Vermont Maple Creemees and Maine Potato Candies, remain uniquely regional. Over time, New England's dessert repertoire has evolved far beyond the old-fashioned buckles, brown betties, and pandowdies of yore to include modern slab pies, snack cakes, even pavlovas. The result is a rich repertoire of flavors that brings out the best in every season.

A Brief History of New England Foodways

The nomadic Native Peoples of the Northeast woodlands built their food cultures around the forest and the seasons, using wild indigenous ingredients like blueberries, cranberries, nuts, and maple sugar; cultivating corn, beans, pumpkins, and squash; as well as catching fish and hunting wild game. The Algonquin tribes that populated the area now known as New England include the Abenaki and Wabanaki (and their many subtribes) to the north and the Mahican, Massachusett, Mohegan, Narragansett, Nipmuc, Pequot, Pocumtuc, Quiripi, and Wampanoag to the south.

Corn, beans, and squash were staples of native cuisine in New England. These crops, known as the Three Sisters, were grown together for mutual benefit. The native tribes dried and ground corn and used it to make little cakes to boil or fry, as well as *nasaump*, a cornmeal porridge with local nuts and berries. Pumpkins and squash were roasted, mashed, and eaten raw. While dessert wasn't part of the native culture, they did have access to the sap of maple trees, which they collected and boiled into maple syrup and sugar. They used the crystallized sugar as a seasoning and preservative for meat and fish like Europeans used salt. They added it to cold water to create a refreshing tonic in the summertime. In the winter, children poured the hot syrup onto snow to create taffy. Sweetness, in moderation, was part of the indigenous diet.

When the British settlers arrived, they brought their stationary agricultural lifestyle. The first cows were brought to Plymouth Colony in 1624. Orchard favorites, apples and pears, were brought by ship as cuttings and soon spread across the region by seed. The colonists also brought an appetite for puddings (the British term for sweet desserts, which range in texture from dense cakes to loose custards). They applied their cooking techniques to the ingredients that were available in their new environment, resulting in a fusion of influences we now recognize as traditional Yankee cookery.

Take one of the earliest New England recipes, known as Indian Pudding. It's essentially an adaptation of English Hasty Pudding, but instead of using scarce imported wheat flour, the British used what was available during the early days of settlement: cornmeal (which they referred to as "Indian" meal). Indeed, corn was one of the first crops the Natives taught the colonists to plant, and the early settlers were unlikely to have survived without it. Four hundred years later, Indian pudding, flavored with warm spices and molasses (or maple syrup) and served with vanilla ice cream is still a much-beloved regional dessert throughout New England, though its name could certainly use an update (page 157).

For a century or more, agriculture continued to play a central role in New England life. Subsistence farming was the typical lifestyle, in spite of the rockiness of the soil. Dairy farms began sprouting up all over the region. New England's sprawling, serpentine coastline was home to a thriving salt industry in Revolutionary times all the way through the Civil War. Back then, salt was in high demand not just for seasoning but also food preservation in the era before refrigeration (particularly for the region's fishing industry). After the Revolutionary War, New England foodways became a way for just-minted Americans to maintain certain traditions while asserting a newfound cultural independence. Dense puddings became cakes. Biscuits became cookies. A new government was born.

Cane sugar has been a valued addition to the New England pantry for hundreds of years. Without it, dessert as a concept certainly wouldn't exist. Cane sugar eventually displaced maple sugar and syrup as the main sweetener in New England because it was cheaper and more plentiful (artificially so, because it was produced using slave labor). Molasses, the syrupy, bittersweet byproduct of sugar-processing, was also used as a cheap sweetener as well as fermented to make rum.

It must be noted how much of a role the sugar trade played in the burgeoning economies of the New England colonies. Sugar, molasses, and rum were important commodities, and New England certainly did profit from slavery through the manufacture and trade of rum. Slaves were shipped from West Africa to the Caribbean sugar islands in exchange for sugar and molasses, which were brought to New England to sell and make rum. The rum was then shipped back to Africa for more slaves. It's up for debate whether our developing sweet tooth drove the economy of sugar or whether the supply fueled our appetites, but it's important to acknowledge this dark side of history.

While agriculture continued, industry was starting to take hold in the cities by the 18th century. The ensuing years saw waves of migration. In the mid-1800s, the Irish arrived en masse during the potato famine, along with smaller numbers of Germans, Scots, and French Canadians, who found work in Boston and the surrounding mill towns. A second wave after the Civil War through the turn of the 20th century brought Russian Jews and Italians in droves, as well as Chinese, Portuguese, Armenians, and Black migrants from the South. Each brought their food traditions with them. More recently, New England has seen an influx of immigrants from Asia, Latin America, and the Caribbean. It will be interesting to see what food traditions develop next.

Like our history, New England food is constantly evolving, striking an ever-changing balance between tradition and rebellion. The common thread is an appreciation for our

natural environment, celebration of our agrarian roots, and a spirit of community and gratitude.

The New England Pantry

The New England pantry might look a little different than one in California or the Deep South. First off, there's bound to be a jug of maple syrup hiding in the back of the refrigerator, or a jar of molasses in a cabinet somewhere. There's also likely to be a box of oats or sack of cornmeal (or both) on the pantry shelves. And no New England spice rack is complete without ground cinnamon, nutmeg, allspice, ginger, and cloves.

The following is a list of products I recommend having on hand for the recipes in this book, as well as some tips for using them to the best effect (see the individual chapters for information on seasonal produce). Like anything else, the better your ingredients, the better your final product will be. I recommend prioritizing ingredients from your local New England foodshed—that is, ingredients produced in or near your own community. Local producers are more likely to have a stake in the region they serve and care more about the quality of their products, the health of the environment, and flavor. Produce and dairy will be fresher, and the money you spend stays in the local economy. That said, use what you like and what your budget allows.

Maple

Made from the sap of sugar maple trees (and others), it can be concentrated into syrup or crystallized into grains of sugar. New Englanders love real maple syrup on their pancakes, but its unique caramelized flavor is good for baking, too. Maple sugar can be substituted wherever brown sugar is called for (be advised: the price differential is significant). While concentrations vary, it generally takes about 40 gallons of sap to make 1 gallon of maple syrup. Look for Grade A syrup and then choose from the following color distinctions: Golden, Amber, Dark, Very Dark. Golden maple syrups are lighter in color and flavor with hints of vanilla. Darker maple syrups have a deeper, more interesting flavor profile, with notes of molasses, coffee, or hazelnut. Maple syrup should always be stored in the refrigerator after opening to preserve its flavor and freshness.

Sugar and Molasses

Granulated sugar is made by evaporating water from the juice of sugarcane and sugar beets until the natural sugars crystallize. The dark, syrupy molasses is then removed to create granulated sugar's snowy white color and neutral taste. Small amounts of molasses are then added back to the white sugar in varying amounts to produce light and dark brown sugar. Coarser raw sugars like demerara or turbinado can be substituted for brown sugar, but I recommend grinding them in a spice grinder first so the granules will be small enough to dissolve. Molasses itself is also used in baking to add bittersweet flavor and moisture to baked goods. Confectioner's sugar is white granulated sugar ground into a fine powder so it dissolves faster.

Honey

Honey is concentrated sugar from flower nectar gathered by honeybees. In return, the bees pollinate the plants. Good pollination is very important for high crop yields, so many farmers keep their own bees. The resulting golden syrup has a distinct flavor that can include floral, herbal, even fruity notes, depending on the types of flowers the bees have visited. You can find it jarred, in squeeze-bottles, or sold in its waxy comb. If the honey recrystallizes in the jar, it's still fine to use. Just gently warm it in the microwave in 20-second bursts and stir.

Dairy

Dairy farming has been an important part of New England's agriculture since colonial times, producing high-quality milk, cream, butter, cheese, yogurt, sour cream, and buttermilk for hundreds of years. While dairy farming is on the decline in the region, there are still many responsible companies and co-ops throughout New England that produce wholesome and delicious dairy products (some organic), including Stonyfield, Cabot, Vermont Creamery, and Kate's. Try to support these local businesses and other small farms if you can.

Butter: Made from churned cream, butter is the backbone of countless amazing desserts. Some recipes, like pies and cobblers, call for cold butter. Others, like brownies, call for melted butter. Still others, like many cakes and cookies, specify cool room-temperature butter. By that, I mean softened to the point that the butter can easily be creamed with an electric mixer, but not so soft that it's greasy, squishy, and half-melted. An hour or two at room temperature is sufficient. Most of my recipes call for unsalted butter so I can control the amount of salt myself, but you can swap in salted butter by reducing the salt in a recipe by ¼ teaspoon per stick if you prefer. Keep in mind that unsalted butter doesn't keep as well as salted butter, so store it in the freezer if you don't plan to use it within a week or two.

Milk: Whole milk is usually best for baking and ice cream because of its rich flavor and 3% milkfat. Low-fat milk (1% and 2%) can also be used in desserts, but it will yield a lighter product. The only exception is pumpkin pie, for which I prefer to use a leaner milk, like 1%, which creates a smoother, denser custard. Avoid skim milk, which contains no fat at all.

Cream: I use heavy cream for most of my baking needs (also known as heavy whipping cream), which contains more fat than light whipping cream. Instead of buying separate half-and-half, I measure out half milk and half cream.

Buttermilk: Real buttermilk is the tangy by-product of the butter-making process. I prefer the taste to cultured buttermilk (essentially lacto-fermented milk). If you can't find real buttermilk like Kate's at your supermarket, you can substitute cultured buttermilk, powdered buttermilk (follow the directions on the package), or use a ratio of 1 tablespoon freshly squeezed lemon juice per 1 cup milk to achieve a similar level of acidity.

Yogurt: Yogurt is another fermented milk product that adds moisture and tang to baked goods. I'm particularly fond of Cabot's whole milk Greek yogurt, which is as thick as sour cream (I tend to use the two interchangeably). If a recipe calls for plain yogurt and all you have is Greek, you can thin it with milk or water to the right consistency. Similarly, if a recipe calls for Greek yogurt and all you have is plain, you can drain the yogurt in a fine-mesh sieve over a bowl overnight to get a thicker product.

Cheese: I use cream cheese, mascarpone, and occasionally quark in my dessert preparations. These are soft, fresh cheeses that add texture and tang to cheesecakes and frostings.

Eggs

You can find fresh eggs at your local farmers' market, farm stand, or even from a friendly neighbor. My local Agway offers them. Basically, anytime I see local eggs for sale, I buy a dozen because I'll always use them. They're the freshest eggs you can buy, and they're fun because they come in all different sizes and colorful shells, from white to brown to light blue to olive green, depending on the breed of the hen. Large eggs are the standard for baking, but if you have a mixed dozen, try to pair the smaller sizes with the extra-large sizes to approximate a large egg. Eggs incorporate best into batters and doughs when they're at room temperature. If you forget to take the eggs out ahead of time, let them sit in a bowl of warm water for 10 or 15 minutes. If you're just learning how to separate eggs, I recommend cracking the egg into your hand and letting the whites slip between your fingers into the bowl. It's much easier than gingerly transferring the yolk from shell to jagged shell. If you pierce the yolk, the fat will contaminate the whites, making them too slippery to whip up into a stable froth.

Cornmeal

Cornmeal was a common substitution for scarce wheat flour in the early days of colonization. It was made by drying the corn kernels and pounding them into a coarse meal using a mortar and pestle. Later, as the region became more industrialized, the corn could be ground in water-powered gristmills. Arguably one of the oldest New England ingredients, cornmeal adds a pleasant rustic texture and sweet flavor to baked goods.

Wheat Flour

We are lucky to have a company in New England that produces high-quality flour. King Arthur Flour is a local, employee-owned company in Norwich, Vermont. Originally established in Boston, the company has been in existence for more than 200 years. I use all-purpose flour for most of my baking, though sometimes I'll add in some whole wheat flour for heartier cakes. When measuring any flour, I recommend using a whisk to fluff it up first before dipping your measuring cup and leveling it off with a knife. This will keep your baked goods nice and light. If you maintain a gluten-free diet, the all-purpose flour in most of these recipes can be replaced measure-for-measure with gluten-free flour with good results.

Oats, Buckwheat, and Barley

Scottish and German settlers are credited with bringing oats to New England in the 1600s as a cereal grain. They stuck because they're tasty, nutritious, and hardy enough to tolerate our cold, wet climate. Rolled oats are made by steaming oat groats and then rolling them into flakes. This helps the oats stay fresh longer and cook faster. In addition to making a delicious hot cereal and granola, oats add texture, whole grain nutrients, and flavor to crisps, crumbles, and cookies. Another grain suited to the New England climate is buckwheat, which, contrary to the name, contains no wheat or gluten at all. It's especially popular in Maine, where a special Acadian variety is grown for *ployes,* a rustic crepe. You can swap in buckwheat flour for 25% of the flour called for in most cake and cookie recipes. Barley was also historically grown in New England. It's one of the main ingredients in Grape-Nuts, a breakfast cereal that became a popular addition to puddings and ice cream throughout the region.

Walnuts

English walnuts are common components of New England baking due to established British trade routes with Asia and the Middle East. Always taste your walnuts before baking to ensure they're fresh—the oils can turn rancid over time. Storing them in the freezer extends their life.

Salt

Sea salt is made by evaporating seawater until the salt becomes so concentrated, it crystallizes. Today salt comes in several different forms and grinds, from tiny grains of table salt, to fine and coarse grains of sea salt, to kosher salt (a coarse and mellow salt best known for koshering meat). For baking, I tend to use finer grinds of salt because they dissolve and disperse more easily, unless I want the occasional burst of salt here and there. Fine sea salt is my favorite, although I do use table salt as well. For stovetop cooking, I find myself reaching for kosher salt or fine sea salt. When making substitutions, keep in mind that the size of the grind affects how many crystals fit in your measuring spoon. A teaspoon of fine sea salt will pack together more tightly and therefore be saltier than a teaspoon of coarse sea salt.

Spices

What would New England desserts be without pumpkin spice? More specifically, cinnamon, nutmeg, allspice, ginger, cloves, even mace (the funny seed coating that surrounds nutmeg). At one time, spices were so valuable in Europe, they were used as currency. Many were treasured for their medicinal value as well as their flavor. The medieval spice trade brought these fragrant powders from their native homes in Asia, Africa, and the Middle East to Europe and the New World, where they make everything taste better (almost). It has often been suggested that you replace your spices every year because they lose their potency over time, but that can get awfully expensive. Instead, if your spices have been sitting around for a while, do what I do and just increase the amounts to your taste.

Vanilla and Rum

Vanilla, native to Central and South America, is one of the most popular (and expensive) flavors of all time. The extract is indispensable in the kitchen, gently scenting cakes, boosting chocolate flavor, and standing on its own in ice cream. I prefer real vanilla extract to artificial, but use what you like and what fits your budget. Rum, quite plentiful in old New England, was often used as a flavoring in desserts. I use dark rum for the deep, caramelized flavor that gets imparted from spending time in charred oak casks.

Chocolate

Another indispensable baking ingredient is chocolate. In fact, chocolate chip cookies were invented in New England. Chocolate comes from the bean of the cacao plant, native to Central and South America. The beans are fermented, dried, roasted, then ground into a brown melty liquid called chocolate liquor. This nonalcoholic liquid consists of smooth cocoa butter and the bitter cocoa solids that give chocolate its flavor. Unsweetened chocolate is 100% chocolate liquor with no milk or sugar added. Bittersweet chocolate is slightly sweetened and contains up to 75% chocolate liquor. Semisweet chocolate usually falls between 35–60% chocolate liquor. And milk chocolate is sweeter still, with 10–25% chocolate liquor, depending on whether it's produced in the United States or Europe. White chocolate is cocoa butter without the chocolate liquor, mixed with lots of sugar, milk, and vanilla. Excellent block chocolate brands at your average supermarket are Baker's (this Boston-based company was the first to produce chocolate in the country) and Ghirardelli, but I'd also encourage you to seek out Callebaut, Valrhona, Guittard, and Lindt. While chocolate chips are undeniably convenient (my favorites are Ghirardelli bittersweet chips), they do contain additional ingredients to allow them to hold their form. For purer chocolate that you plan to melt, consider chopping bar or block chocolate.

Cocoa Powder

Unsweetened cocoa powder used for baking (as opposed to making hot cocoa) comes in two varieties: natural and Dutch-process. I recommend stocking both. Dutch-process cocoa powder is treated to remove some of its natural acidity, resulting in a deeper, darker chocolate flavor and color. Natural cocoa powder is just that—it retains its natural acidity. The two cannot be used interchangeably in batters that require chemical leavening. Natural cocoa powder's acidity reacts with baking soda, while Dutch-process cocoa needs the help of baking powder to create a reaction. Ghirardelli and Hershey's are fine natural cocoas most supermarkets stock that won't break the bank. For a next-level option, try Penzeys (which can be ordered online). For Dutch-process cocoa, I recommend Droste or Guittard Red Cocoa, which is carried by some supermarkets, or Rodelle (which can be ordered online). I recommend sifting cocoa powder to eliminate any pesky lumps.

Malted Milk Powder

Best known for its old-fashioned addition to milk shakes and frappes, malted milk powder adds a toasty, sweet flavor reminiscent of malted milk balls. What the heck is malted milk, you ask? It's basically evaporated milk powder mixed with wheat flour and dried, sprouted barley. Sounds awful, tastes great. If you can't find brands like Carnation or Horlick's in your grocery store (look for it near the powdered milk), you can find it online. Do not substitute chocolate Ovaltine—it's not the same. (*Note:* Malted milk contains gluten.)

Spring

*S*pring is a time of unbridled excitement in New England. Only after the long, cold winter can you truly appreciate the first signs of spring: crocuses peeking out of the snow, the first robin, a sudden, unexpected warm spell. It's a slow start, to be sure. First comes the wind. Then the rain (and maybe also snow, just to keep you guessing). Then, out of a thick and luxurious mud, the greening of the landscape begins. Trees bud and unfurl their leaves, apple and cherry trees blossom, fat tulips defy gravity on their slender stems. Around here, the white-throated sparrow, with its high-pitched "Old Sam Peabody, Peabody, Peabody" reminds me to start planting my garden. My sons and I head out to the woods with boots and binoculars in search of migrating birds, salamanders, and rare mushrooms.

Even before the calendar turns to spring, when those first warming days bump up against cold winter nights, the first trickle of maple sap signals spring's stealthy approach. The change in pressure causes the sugar-rich sap in the trees to move from the roots to the tips of their branches during the day, stimulating leaf growth, then back down to the roots again at night. February through April, depending on the latitude and elevation, you're likely to find maple trees all over New England sporting metal buckets and spiles for collecting maple sap. This sap is collected, boiled down, and bottled, often in sugar shacks, tiny cabins billowing telltale steam across the landscape.

By the time spring arrives in earnest, the seasonal larder is nearly bare. We've had our fill of heavy winter food, but local strawberries are still weeks, if not months away. This is when local bakers get creative, making good use of the region's farm-fresh eggs, rich cream, fresh butter, and hearty whole grains, like oats, cornmeal, buckwheat, and barley. April showers plant the seeds of summer in our minds. Come May and June, we nearly burst with anticipation as rhubarb's green stalks emerge, blushing pink to crimson, and the first early strawberries whet our appetite for summer's bounty.

Parsnips

Spring-dug parsnips—thick, straw-colored taproots similar to carrots—are one of the earliest pleasures of springtime. Farmers will often leave part of their fall harvest in the ground to overwinter, which concentrates the sugars, yielding an even sweeter flavor. You might not think of the humble parsnip as the basis for dessert, but consider how much we love carrots in cake—parsnips are just as good. If you're lucky, you'll stumble upon a stall with spring-dug parsnips at the season's earliest farmers' markets, and then you can try them in the Maple Brown Butter Parsnip Cake (page 21).

Rhubarb

This quirky member of the buckwheat family is technically a vegetable, but it's eaten like a fruit in pies and jam. Sometimes called "pie-plant" in old cookbooks, rhubarb's stalks are edible and delicious. They range in color from green to pink to candy-apple red based on variety, not ripeness. Rhubarb is tart and bracing raw, but pleasantly sweet when sugared. It's traditionally paired with strawberries in pies and crisps, but rhubarb is plenty satisfying all on its own. In fact, many New Englanders prefer it that way (including me). Native to Asia, rhubarb was brought to New England by the British settlers, and its ability to withstand the harsh New England winters continues to make it a popular garden plant. Rhubarb is often sold with the leaves removed since they contain toxic oxalic acid. Choose crisp, unblemished stalks with ends that look moist, not woody or dry, and put them to work in Rhubarb Ginger Crumb Cake (page 28), Rhubarb Oat Crisp (page 22), and Rhubarb Ripple Ice Cream (page 4).

Strawberries

Long-awaited strawberries mark the transition from spring to summer here in New England, where they're most often paired with shortcake and cream (page 26). A member of the rose family, strawberries grew wild across the Americas and Europe. Most commercial strawberries these days are hybrids of the North American wild strawberry species, *Fragaria virginiana*, but everbearing strawberry plants grow wild throughout New England and produce small fruits all season long. Supermarket strawberries are often sprayed with chemicals and picked underripe so the fruits don't get bruised during transport. Whenever possible, opt for local strawberries that are picked at peak ripeness and are less likely to be sprayed. The season is short, so act fast. Choose bright, plump berries with the green caps still attached. Don't be tempted by size—smaller berries are often the most flavorful. While strawberries are irresistible straight out of hand, try to save some for the Strawberry Buttermilk Cupcakes (page 19) and Strawberry Rosewater Sorbet (page 32).

Rhubarb Ripple Ice Cream

I get a little obsessed with rhubarb in the springtime, putting it in just about everything, including places it doesn't belong. But rhubarb and vanilla are a natural pairing, and this ice cream is a winner. Look for rhubarb that's more rosy than green to create a pretty pink ribbon running through your frozen custard. If your rhubarb is green, there's nothing wrong with it— that's just the variety. If you like, you can punch up the color with a few raspberries, which will improve the visual appeal. Any extra rhubarb jam can be used as a topping for ice cream or stored in the refrigerator to be spread on toast or stirred into yogurt. Covered in the refrigerator, it will keep for 2–3 weeks. Because this ice cream has a cooked custard base that needs to chill before churning and needs plenty of time to freeze, try to make it at least a day before you plan to serve it. For tips on making homemade ice cream, see page 189.

For the vanilla base:

2 cups heavy cream, divided

2 large egg yolks

1 cup milk (preferably whole, but not skim)

¾ cup granulated sugar

Pinch of salt

2 teaspoons vanilla extract or vanilla bean paste

For the rhubarb ripple:

½ pound rhubarb, chopped into ½-inch pieces (about 2 cups)

1 cup granulated sugar, divided

1 tablespoon water

1 tablespoon lemon juice, freshly squeezed (about ½ lemon)

For the ice cream base, set a strainer in a large bowl near the stove and add 1 cup of cream.

In a medium saucepan off heat, whisk the yolks, then slowly whisk in the milk. Gradually whisk in the sugar. Stir in the remaining cream and salt.

Cook over medium heat, stirring constantly with a wooden spoon, until it comes to a bare simmer, 8–12 minutes. Pour the hot mixture into the strainer bowl. Remove the strainer and stir in the vanilla. Let cool to room temperature, then cover and refrigerate until cold, 6 hours or overnight.

Meanwhile, for the rhubarb ripple, combine the chopped rhubarb, 1 tablespoon of the sugar, and water in a medium saucepan over medium-high heat. Stir the rhubarb as it simmers and softens, 5–6 minutes. Bring the mixture to a full rolling boil and add the rest of the sugar all at once. Bring back to a boil and boil hard for 1 minute. Remove from the heat and stir in the lemon juice. Transfer to a bowl and cool to room temperature. Cover with plastic wrap pressed right against the surface. Refrigerate until cold.

Pour the chilled ice cream base into an ice cream machine and follow the manufacturer's instructions. Spoon into a freezer-safe container, adding thin layers of rhubarb jam between the scoops. Freeze until firm, at least 6 hours. When you scoop out the ice cream, the layers of rhubarb will form pretty ripples.

Note: For instructions on how to make ice cream without a machine, see page 190.

Maine Whoopie Pies

These old-fashioned chocolate cake sandwiches with marshmallow filling bring out the kid in all of us. They're the official state treat of Maine, where they hold a Whoopie Pie Festival in Dover-Foxcroft. The original whoopie pies were made with lard or vegetable shortening, but I prefer to use butter. Dutch-process cocoa provides the richest flavor and darkest color. For the cloudlike filling, I call for locally made Marshmallow Fluff (manufactured by Durkee-Mower in Lynn, Massachusetts), but I've also provided the option to make your own marshmallow cream from whipped egg whites.

MAKES ABOUT 1 DOZEN

For the cakes:

4 ounces unsalted butter, at cool room temperature

1 cup light brown sugar, firmly packed

2 large eggs, at room temperature

1 teaspoon vanilla extract

2 cups all-purpose flour

½ cup Dutch-process cocoa powder, sifted

1 teaspoon baking powder

1 teaspoon baking soda

1 teaspoon salt

1 cup milk

1 tablespoon white vinegar

Preheat the oven to 375°F. Grease or line two cookie sheets with parchment paper.

For the cakes, cream the butter and brown sugar with an electric mixer (preferably fitted with a paddle attachment) for 2–3 minutes until fluffy, starting on low speed then increasing to medium-high. Scrape down the sides and bottom of the bowl as needed. Add the eggs, one at a time, mixing well after each addition. Add the vanilla and beat 3–4 minutes more on medium while preparing the dry ingredients. The mixture should be light in color and very fluffy.

Meanwhile, sift together the flour, cocoa powder, baking powder, baking soda, and salt in a medium bowl. Add half of the dry ingredients to the butter base and mix on low speed just until combined. Stir the milk and vinegar together. Gradually add the milk mixture down the side of the bowl with the mixer running on low. Turn the mixer off and add the rest of the dry ingredients. Mix on low just until combined. The batter should be thick enough to hold its shape when scooped, slumping just a little. Drop the batter in heaping tablespoon-sized dollops spaced 2–3 inches apart (a 1-ounce cookie scoop works great here).

Bake 9–11 minutes until the centers are set and spring back when gently pressed. For best results, bake one cookie sheet at a time on the center rack. Let sit on the hot pan for 5 minutes before transferring to racks to cool. Repeat with the second and third batches.

For the filling:

6 ounces unsalted butter, at cool room temperature

3 cups confectioner's sugar, sifted, divided

2 teaspoons vanilla extract

Pinch of salt

1 cup Marshmallow Fluff

1 tablespoon heavy cream (if needed)

For the filling, cream the butter on medium speed with an electric mixer until smooth. Beat in half of the confectioner's sugar until fluffy. Scrape down the sides and bottom of the bowl as needed. Mix in the vanilla and salt. Beat in the rest of the confectioner's sugar. Add the Marshmallow Fluff and mix just until blended. Although not always necessary, you can dribble in and mix up to 1 tablespoon heavy cream to get the desired consistency.

To assemble, wait until the cakes are fully cooled. Match up similarly sized cakes. Spoon a heaping tablespoon of filling and place in the center of the flat side of one of the cakes (again, a 1-ounce cookie scoop is the perfect tool). Sandwich another on top, and gently press until the filling reaches the edges. Repeat for the rest. Store in an airtight container in the refrigerator for up to 3 days or freeze. Enjoy cold or at room temperature.

The New England Connection: Whoopie Pies

Whoopie pies, which have been a Maine tradition for at least a century, were most likely brought to New England by German immigrants. Labadie's Bakery in Lewiston, Maine, has been producing them since 1925. They're also popular in Pennsylvania among the Amish and Pennsylvania Dutch, where they're often called "gobs." The name "whoopie pies" came from the Berwick Cake Company in Roxbury, Massachusetts. They had been offering a whoopie pie–like confection for years, but it wasn't selling. When the Broadway show *Whoopee!* came to Boston in the fall of 1929, Berwick suggested having the actors toss "Whoopee!" pies into the audience at curtain call. No surprise—they were a hit! Berwick later patented the name "whoopie pie" with a slight change in spelling to avoid copyright infringement, but the original "whoopee!" spelling can still be faintly seen on one of the old buildings in Dudley Square (the bakery closed in 1977). The popularity of the treats and the show cemented the name and most certainly helped to spread word of the once strictly regional dessert.

Marshmallow Cream

If you don't have a tub of Marshmallow Fluff handy, here's how to make it yourself. When separating the eggs, it's important that the yolks don't break or it will prevent the whites from whipping properly. Cream of tartar, the powdered acid residue from wine barrels, helps the egg whites whip up to a larger volume and provides stability.

MAKES ABOUT 2 CUPS

2 large egg whites
½ cup granulated sugar
¼ teaspoon cream of tartar
Pinch of salt
1 teaspoon vanilla

Set a small saucepan with an inch of water to boil. In a large metal mixing bowl (or the bowl of a stand mixer), whisk the egg whites, sugar, cream of tartar, and salt. Set the bowl over the pan of boiling water (the bottom of the bowl should not be touching the water) and whisk constantly for about 3 minutes, until the sugar dissolves. (You can check by rubbing a small amount of the hot mixture between your fingers to check for grittiness.) Remove from the heat and whisk in the vanilla. With an electric mixer, beat the mixture on high speed for 3–5 minutes until stiff and glossy. Store the unused portion in a jar or bowl, covered, in the refrigerator for up to 2 days. Use for Fluffernutter sandwiches (peanut butter and Fluff).

Maple Cheesecake

Maple lovers swoon over this rich, decadent dessert. If you can't find maple sugar at your local grocery store, you can purchase it online (I recommend Coombs Family Farms in Brattleboro, Vermont). In a pinch, you can substitute light brown sugar. For a smoother cheesecake, let your cream cheese sit out at room temperature for several hours ahead of time. Serve plain or with a seasonal fruit sauce, like Strawberry Rhubarb (page 39) or Blueberry (page 83).

SERVES 12–16

For the crust:

4 tablespoons unsalted butter, melted

1 heaping cup graham cracker crumbs, finely ground (about 4 ounces)

Pinch of salt

For the filling:

1 cup fine maple sugar

4 (8-ounce) packages cream cheese (not light or whipped), at cool room temperature

¼ cup maple syrup (the darker, the better)

½ teaspoon vanilla extract

4 large eggs, at room temperature

Preheat the oven to 275°F. Grease a 9-inch springform pan.

Melt the butter in a medium bowl in the microwave (or a small saucepan). Stir in the cookie crumbs and salt until evenly moistened. Press into the bottom only of the prepared pan. Bake 10 minutes. Let cool.

Meanwhile, if your maple sugar is coarser than regular sugar, grind it in a food processor for several minutes until finely ground. (If you don't have a food processor, you can use a mortar and pestle in batches.)

Beat the cream cheese and maple sugar with an electric mixer (preferably fitted with a paddle attachment) starting on low speed, then increasing to medium. Beat until smooth and the sugar dissolves (but no more than 2 or 3 minutes to prevent air bubbles), scraping down the sides and bottom of the bowl as needed. Mix in the maple syrup, vanilla, and eggs all at once, and beat on low speed just until combined. Scrape down the bowl and mix briefly once more. Pour the batter onto the crust.

Bake 1 hour on the middle rack (the cake may still be sunken in the center). Turn off the heat and let it sit in the oven with the door *closed* for 2 hours, until the center has risen, is set, and the oven has mostly cooled. Remove the cake from the oven and let it cool completely to room temperature before placing it in the refrigerator for at least 5–6 hours before serving.

Note: For a lighter-textured cheesecake, put a roasting pan with ½ inch of water in it on the bottom rack of the oven during baking.

Strawberry Rhubarb Tarts

I love rustic, open-faced tarts for their personality and shatteringly crisp crust. Where I live in Massachusetts, late May through June is the time for these pretty little tarts, when the rhubarb is up but strawberries haven't yet reached peak shortcake numbers. Often, it's my first entry into pie season. Luckily, the heat isn't usually too oppressive to have the oven on and, if I'm honest, I'd still make these in a heat wave. For rhubarb purists, you can also make them without strawberries (add a tablespoon or two of additional sugar or heavy cream to the filling to tame the tartness).

MAKES 2 9-INCH TARTS

For the crust:

2 cups all-purpose flour

1 tablespoon granulated sugar

1 teaspoon kosher salt

1½ sticks (¾ cup) cold unsalted butter, cut into 12 pieces

6–8 tablespoons ice water

For the filling:

1 pound rhubarb, cut into ½-inch pieces

12 ounces strawberries, hulled, halved, or quartered depending on size

1 teaspoon vanilla extract

1 teaspoon lemon juice, freshly squeezed

¾ cup light brown sugar, packed

¼ cup cornstarch

Pinch of cinnamon

Preheat the oven to 400°F. Grease or line two rimmed sheet pans with parchment paper.

For the crust, combine the flour, sugar, and salt in the bowl of a food processor. Add the cold butter and process 10–15 seconds, until the butter pieces stop jumping around like popcorn. Add 4 tablespoons (¼ cup) ice water and process 2–3 seconds. Add additional water 1 tablespoon at a time, pulsing the motor 5–6 times to mix. You may only need 1 or 2 additional tablespoons of water, or you may require all 4, but only add what you need. Stop when the dough starts to come together and holds its shape when gently squeezed. (If you don't have a food processor, you can cut the butter into small pea-sized pieces with a pastry blender, fork and knife, or your fingers.)

Gather the dough together, gently kneading once or twice to make sure it holds together. Form into two thick disks about the same size, and wrap in waxed paper, plastic wrap, or reusable wraps. Let them rest in the refrigerator 20–30 minutes.

For the filling, combine the rhubarb and strawberries in a large bowl. Add the vanilla and lemon juice. In a separate small bowl, mix the brown sugar, cornstarch, and cinnamon together. Set aside.

Flour your counter and rolling pin well. Roll out one disk of dough to 10 or 11 inches in diameter (slightly less than ¼ inch thick). Transfer the dough to the prepared pan by loosening

For preparation:

1 egg, beaten

Granulated sugar, for
  sprinkling

the dough from the counter a little at a time with a bench scraper or spatula, and draping it over the rolling pin. Using a slotted spoon, transfer half of the fruit to the center of the dough, leaving an inch or two margin around the edge. Sprinkle half of the sugar mixture over the fruit. Fold over the edges in short segments to form a rough circle or whatever other shape you'd like. Brush the dough with beaten egg mixed with a teaspoon of water and sprinkle with sugar. Repeat with the second disk of dough along with the remaining fruit and sugar mixture.

Bake 35–40 minutes, until the crust is golden brown and the filling is bubbly and thick. Let cool at least a half hour so the filling can set. Serve with Connecticut Valley Vanilla Ice Cream or Maine Buttermilk and Sea Salt Ice Cream. Pies and tarts are best served the day they're made, as the crust softens over time, but they can be refrigerated for a day or two and eaten for breakfast like danish.

Salted Oat and Walnut Sandies

Salty and sweet, buttery and crisp, these simple, unassuming cookies are surprisingly addictive. They're also endlessly versatile. Crumble them over ice cream for an easy sundae topping or use them instead of graham crackers for a cheesecake crust. If you're a cookie dough fiend like I am, you can indulge without fear—there's no raw egg in the dough. Sure, you can gild the lily with chocolate chunks or dried cranberries or whatever else your heart desires. But me, I'm flying under the radar with these so I can finally get some cookies to myself around here.

MAKES ABOUT 2 DOZEN

- 1½ sticks (¾ cup) unsalted butter, at cool room temperature
- ¾ cup light brown sugar, firmly packed
- 1 cup all-purpose flour
- ½ teaspoon baking soda
- 1 teaspoon sea salt or kosher salt
- ⅔ cup rolled oats
- ½ cup chopped walnuts

In a medium bowl, cream the butter and sugar with an electric mixer until creamy, 1–2 minutes. Add the flour, baking soda, and salt, and mix on low speed just until combined. Add the oats and walnuts, and mix until dispersed. Press the mixture into a log 2 inches in diameter and wrap it in waxed paper or plastic wrap. Refrigerate at least 1 hour and up to 2 days until firm.

Preheat the oven to 350°F. Grease or line two cookie sheets with parchment paper.

Unwrap the dough and, with a sharp knife, cut into ¼- to ½-inch slices and set on the prepared pans. Bake 17–19 minutes until golden. Let sit 5 minutes on the hot cookie sheets before transferring to a wire rack to cool.

Boston Cream Pie

As New Englanders know, Boston Cream Pie is not a pie at all, but rather a sponge cake split across the equator, filled with vanilla custard, and topped with a chocolate glaze. The original cake was created at Boston's Parker House Hotel in 1855 (now Omni Parker House). The cake and custard are best made a day ahead to allow for proper chilling. After that, the assembly comes together quickly. To up your game, try brushing the cut sponge cake with Bailey's Irish Cream before assembling for a boozy Irish twist. Or sub in Amaretto, Frangelico, or Kahlua. A sprinkling of flaky sea salt on top makes this cake really sparkle.

SERVES 8–12

For the cake:

6 large eggs (2 yolks reserved for the filling)

¼ teaspoon table salt

1 cup granulated sugar, divided in half

1 cup all-purpose flour

4 tablespoons unsalted butter, melted

1 teaspoon vanilla extract

Preheat the oven to 350°F. Grease the bottom and sides of one 9-inch high-sided springform pan (grease all the way up the sides), or two shorter 9-inch cake pans. Line the bottoms with parchment paper rounds.

For the cake, start by carefully separating the eggs (set aside two yolks for the filling). Add the whites to the bowl of a stand mixer (fitted with the whisk attachment) or other large bowl for a handheld mixer. Beat the whites on medium speed until foamy, about 30 seconds. With the mixer running, gradually add ½ cup of the sugar and all of the salt. Beat on medium-high for 4–6 minutes until firm peaks form (peaks that hold their shape without the tips drooping).

Meanwhile, whisk 4 egg yolks by hand in a large bowl with the remaining ½ cup of sugar. Continue whisking about 2 minutes until the mixture thickens, lightens in color, and forms thick ribbons that take a second to sink back into the bowl.

With a rubber spatula, add a scoop of the beaten egg whites to the yolk mixture and stir until combined. Place the rest of the whites on top. Gently fold then whites into the mixture, using the spatula to lift the yolk mixture from the bottom of the bowl, carefully depositing it on top, and rotating the bowl a quarter turn. Repeat until nearly combined. In three or four batches, sprinkle the flour on top and fold it in gently, trying to keep as much air as possible in the mixture. When mostly mixed, fold in the melted butter and vanilla until all the ingredients are fully incorporated, about 10–15 more strokes. Scrape the batter into the prepared pan(s), spreading the batter all the way to the sides.

For the filling:

½ cup granulated sugar

¼ cup cornstarch

¼ teaspoon table salt

2 yolks (reserved from the cake)

1¾ cups milk (not skim)

2 tablespoons unsalted butter

2 teaspoons vanilla extract

For the glaze:

¼ cup heavy cream

½ cup semisweet or bittersweet chocolate chips or chopped chocolate

For assembly:

3 tablespoons Bailey's Irish Cream, Amaretto, Kahlua, or Frangelico (optional)

Flaky sea salt for finishing (optional)

Bake about 20–25 minutes, until golden on top and the centers are set (you can test with a toothpick to make sure there's no raw batter). Remove from the oven and let cool fully.

For the filling, whisk together the sugar, cornstarch, and salt in a medium saucepan until uniformly powdery. In a small bowl, whisk together the 2 reserved yolks and ¼ cup of the milk. Add the yolk mixture to the pot and whisk until smooth. Gradually whisk in the rest of the milk. Set the pan over medium heat and cook, whisking constantly, until it thickens like pudding, 5–7 minutes. Remove from the heat and switch to a wooden spoon to stir in the butter and vanilla. Transfer to a heatproof bowl and cover the surface with plastic wrap to prevent a skin from forming (cut a small hole in the plastic for a steam vent). Let cool at room temperature and then chill in the refrigerator 6 hours or overnight.

Just before assembling, make the glaze. Combine the cream and chocolate chips in a small heatproof bowl or measuring cup. Heat in the microwave in 30-second increments, stirring in between, until melted and smooth. (You can also heat the cream and chocolate in a small saucepan on the stove over very low heat. If it overheats and splits, add a splash of milk and whisk off heat until it comes together again.) Let cool completely at room temperature. (If it sits too long and solidifies, reheat gently in the microwave on low heat, stirring in 15-second increments and let cool to room temperature again.)

To assemble, split the cake in half horizontally with a serrated knife (if you used a springform pan) and remove the parchment paper. Brush the cut sides of the cake with liquor if desired. Place the bottom of the cake, cut-side-up on the serving plate. Spread the custard on top, thickly, to about ½-inch from the edge. Place the top half of the cake cut-side-down. Once centered, press gently until the custard comes right to the edge.

Once the glaze has cooled fully, check that it has thickened slightly but is still fluid enough to pour. Pour it over the top of the cake all at once so it spills over the sides (you can use a cake spatula if necessary). Let the ganache firm up a bit in the refrigerator before sprinkling on the sea salt. Keep refrigerated until ready to serve. Leftovers can be stored, covered, in the refrigerator 2–3 days.

Strawberry Buttermilk Cupcakes

Flour Bakery has become a Boston institution, and I'm obsessed with, of all things, Joanne Chang's vanilla cupcakes. They are, to me, the perfect cupcake, and reflect the skill of the pastry chef the same way a simple broth is the measure of a classically trained French chef. I've barely altered the cupcake recipe at all except to add a dollop of fresh strawberry jam to the centers and an American-style strawberry frosting on top, because strawberry season is short and who can resist pink cupcakes? For a manageable workflow, make the jam the day before (you can always substitute your favorite farmers' market jam to save on time). Don't be alarmed by the white wine vinegar in the frosting—it's there to balance the sweetness and bring out the strawberry flavor—but if you don't have it, you can leave it out. This frosting recipe makes enough to pipe tall decorative rosettes atop your cupcakes, bakery-style, but if you're only planning to add a schmear, consider halving the recipe. Be sure to stop by Flour Bakery for cookies, cakes, and all manner of tempting pastries whenever you're in town.

MAKES 18 CUPCAKES

For the strawberry jam:

1 pound chopped ripe
strawberries (3 cups)

1 cup granulated sugar,
divided

½ lemon (seeds removed)

For the cupcakes:

2 cups all-purpose flour

1⅓ cups granulated sugar

1 teaspoon baking powder

½ teaspoon baking soda

½ teaspoon salt

1 stick (½ cup) unsalted
butter, at cool room
temperature

½ cup vegetable oil

2 large eggs, at room
temperature

2 large yolks

1 teaspoon vanilla extract

⅔ cup buttermilk, well
shaken

For the jam, add the strawberries, 1 tablespoon of the sugar, and the lemon half to a small saucepan. Cook over medium heat for 5 minutes until the berries release their juices. Reduce the heat to low and continue simmering 10 minutes more, mashing the berries against the side of the pan until the berries break down. Increase the heat and bring to a hard boil. Stir in the rest of the sugar all at once. Bring back to a hard boil and continue boiling 2–3 minutes, stirring occasionally, until thick and syrupy. Let cool completely.

Preheat the oven to 350°F. Line 2 standard cupcake pans with 18 liners.

For the cupcakes, combine the flour, sugar, baking powder, baking soda, and salt in the bowl of a stand mixer fitted with the paddle attachment. Blend on low speed. Add the butter, a few tablespoons at a time, mixing on low for a minute after each addition, 3–5 minutes total, until incorporated. In a small bowl, whisk together the oil, eggs, yolks, and vanilla. With the mixer on low, pour it into the butter mixture, scraping down the sides and bottom of the bowl as needed. Then add the buttermilk. Mix just until combined. Divide the batter into the cupcake pan, filling them ⅔ of the way to the top (a 1.5-ounce cookie scoop works perfectly for this).

For the frosting:

4 ounces strawberries, hulled (4–6 medium strawberries)

2 sticks (1 cup) unsalted butter, at cool room temperature

4 ounces (½ cup) cream cheese, at cool room temperature

5 cups confectioner's sugar

2 teaspoons white wine vinegar or Champagne vinegar

½ teaspoon vanilla extract

Dash of salt

For garnish:

1 quart small strawberries (optional)

Bake 25–28 minutes until the centers spring back when gently pressed. Let cool completely before frosting.

For the frosting, puree the strawberries in a food processor until very smooth. Measure out ¼ cup of strawberry puree (2 tablespoons if making a half-batch of frosting). Beat the butter and cream cheese with an electric mixer (preferably fitted with the paddle attachment) on medium to medium-high for 1 minute. Add half the confectioner's sugar on low speed, scraping down the bottom and sides of the bowl as needed. Add the white wine vinegar, vanilla, and salt, and mix well. Add the remaining confectioner's sugar and beat until smooth. Add the strawberry puree 1 tablespoon at a time, beating well after each addition. (You might be tempted to add more strawberry puree, but I would advise against it—butter frostings tend to curdle when too much liquid is added.) Frosting can be refrigerated for 1–2 days before frosting. Let it come to cool room temperature first.

To assemble the cupcakes, first cut out a little plug of cake from the top of each (about ½ inch wide and ½ inch deep). Fill each well with a teaspoon-sized dollop of strawberry jam. (Keep the remaining jam in a covered jar in the refrigerator for toast, yogurt, or future cupcakes for up to 1 month.) Use a piping bag fitted with a decorative tip to pipe the frosting onto the cooled cupcakes, or use a resealable bag with the corner snipped, or spread with a spatula. Top with whole or halved strawberries, if desired. Cupcakes should be kept refrigerated and can be stored covered for 2–3 days.

Maple Brown Butter Parsnip Cake

The humble parsnip is often overlooked in favor of carrots. But parsnips are delicious in cake. What's more, spring-dug parsnips are even sweeter than those harvested early in the fall, because the cold winter temperatures cause their starches to be converted into sugar. When shredding peeled parsnips with a box grater, stop when you hit the tough central core. Turn it to another side and continue grating until you hit the core again. I've iced this cake with an apple cider glaze, but you can also juice a mandarin orange or sub in a tablespoon of coffee for the cider instead.

SERVES 8–12

For the cake:

1½ sticks (¾ cup) unsalted butter

⅔ cup granulated sugar

⅓ cup maple syrup (the darker, the better)

½ teaspoon vanilla extract

2 large eggs, at room temperature

2 cups all-purpose flour

1 teaspoon baking powder

¼ teaspoon baking soda

1 teaspoon ground cinnamon

1 teaspoon ground ginger

½ teaspoon ground nutmeg

Pinch of ground cloves

½ teaspoon salt

½ cup buttermilk, shaken

1 cup shredded parsnips (from about 1 large or 2 medium parsnips)

For the glaze:

½ cup confectioner's sugar

1 tablespoon apple cider

2–3 drops of vanilla extract

Preheat the oven to 350°F. Grease a standard 9½ × 5½-inch loaf pan and line it with parchment paper folded in half. Let the paper hang over the edges for easier lifting.

In a small, heavy-bottomed saucepan, brown the butter over medium-low heat, stirring occasionally, until the butter foams, smells toasty, and the solids at the bottom are deeply browned (not black), 5–10 minutes. (If you have a hard time seeing the color of the butter, spoon some onto a white plate, scraping up the solids from the bottom of the pan.)

In a large bowl, whisk together the brown butter, sugar, maple syrup, and vanilla. Whisk in the eggs, one at a time, until well combined. In a separate medium bowl, whisk together the flour, baking powder, baking soda, all the spices, and salt. With a wooden spoon, stir half of the dry ingredients into the large bowl. Stir in the buttermilk. Add the remaining dry ingredients and mix just until combined. Then stir in the shredded parsnips. Spread the batter in the prepared pan.

Bake 55–60 minutes, until a toothpick inserted into the center comes out with only moist crumbs attached, no raw batter. Let cool completely.

For the glaze, whisk together the confectioner's sugar, cider, and vanilla until smooth. If too runny, add a tablespoon or two of sugar. If too thick, add more cider, a few drops at a time. Drizzle the icing over the cooled cake. Leave the cake uncovered while the icing sets. Once the icing is dry, the cake can be stored, covered, at room temperature for 2–3 days.

Rhubarb Oat Crisp

Strawberry and rhubarb are a classic pairing, but sometimes rhubarb likes to stand alone. A pinch of cinnamon and a touch of vanilla temper rhubarb's wildness, while the buttery, crisp topping scattered with wholesome oats provides rustic texture. Serve this sweet-tart dessert with a scoop of Connecticut Valley Vanilla Ice Cream (page 193) or Maine Buttermilk and Sea Salt Ice Cream (page 204). Or you can simply drizzle some cold heavy cream right over the top of the warm crisp and call it a day.

SERVES 6–8

For the filling:

1 pound rhubarb, cut into ¾-inch pieces

¾ cup granulated sugar

2 tablespoons all-purpose flour

1 tablespoon lemon juice, freshly squeezed

½ teaspoon vanilla extract

Pinch of cinnamon

For the topping:

⅓ cup all-purpose flour

⅓ cup light brown sugar, firmly packed

¼ teaspoon fine sea salt

6 tablespoons cold unsalted butter, cut into 6 pieces

¼ cup rolled oats

Preheat the oven to 350°F. Butter the inside of an 8 × 8-inch baking dish or 9-inch pie plate.

For the filling, combine the rhubarb, sugar, flour, lemon juice, vanilla, and cinnamon in the prepared dish. Set aside.

For the topping, combine the flour, brown sugar, and salt in the bowl of a food processor. Process briefly to combine. Add the butter and pulse until the mixture is crumbly. Stir in the oats with a spoon. (You can also make the topping by hand, cutting the butter into the dry ingredients with your hands or a pastry blender.)

Scatter the mixture over the rhubarb and bake 50–55 minutes, or until the top is golden brown and the rhubarb juices are bubbly. Remove from the oven and let it cool slightly before serving.

Leftovers can be stored, covered, in the refrigerator 2–3 days. Reheat in the oven or microwave (if the latter, the topping will lose its crispness).

Salted + Malted Brownies

These are the brownies of my dreams: chewy and deeply chocolatey with a hint of malt and spark of salt. The shiny tops remind me of boxed brands (they come together almost as quickly), but the flavor is better than most. Eat them right out of hand or create a brownie sundae with your favorite ice cream. If you can't find malted milk powder, just replace it with ¼ cup additional light brown sugar.

MAKES 9 LARGE OR 16 SMALL
BROWNIES (THE RECIPE CAN
BE DOUBLED FOR A 9 × 13-
INCH PAN)

4 tablespoons unsalted
butter

½ cup light brown sugar,
firmly packed

½ cup semisweet
chocolate chips

2 large eggs

1¼ cups confectioner's
sugar

¼ cup vegetable oil

¼ cup hot water (not
boiling)

1 teaspoon vanilla extract

½ cup all-purpose flour

½ cup unsweetened cocoa
powder (not Dutch-
process)

⅓ cup malted milk powder

½ teaspoon kosher salt

¼ teaspoon baking soda

Preheat the oven to 350°F. Grease an 8 × 8-inch pan or line with parchment paper.

Melt the butter in a large microwave-safe bowl in the microwave. Add the brown sugar and heat 1 minute until hot. (Or you can melt the butter in a small saucepan, add the sugar, cook 1 minute, then remove from the heat.) Add the chocolate chips and let sit 1 minute to soften. Stir well until the chocolate is melted and smooth. Let it cool a bit.

Whisk in the eggs, one at a time, until well blended. Add the confectioner's sugar, oil, water, and vanilla. Stir with a wooden spoon until combined. Then add the flour, cocoa powder, malted milk powder, salt, and baking soda. Mix just until combined. Scrape the batter into the prepared pan, nudging it into the corners until even.

Bake 32–38 minutes until the edges are set and a toothpick inserted into the center comes out with a few moist crumbs. Let cool completely. They will become chewier as they sit. Store in an airtight container at room temperature for up to 1 week.

Classic Strawberry Shortcake

While I can't be certain exactly where this classic American dessert originated, it certainly has the hallmarks of a New England dessert: just-picked strawberries in their own flavorful syrup; rustic, not-too-sweet shortcakes for soaking up said juices; and a pillow of fresh whipped cream. Together they combine to create dessert perfection. What's clear is that shortcakes are a British contribution. The rest was up to season, circumstance, and the anticipation of summer after a long winter. No one in their right mind should ever let strawberry season pass them by without having strawberry shortcake grace the table at least once.

SERVES 6–8

For the topping:

2 quarts fresh strawberries, hulled, sliced

1/3 cup granulated sugar

For the shortcake:

2 cups all-purpose flour

1/4 cup granulated sugar

1 tablespoon baking powder

1/2 teaspoon baking soda

1/2 teaspoon salt

4 tablespoons unsalted butter, cut into 4 pieces

1 cup buttermilk (or 1 tablespoon lemon juice, freshly squeezed, stirred into 1 cup milk)

For the cream:

1 pint heavy cream

2 tablespoons confectioner's sugar

Vanilla extract, to taste

Preheat the oven to 450°F. Grease a cookie sheet or line it with parchment paper.

In a medium bowl, gently stir together the sliced strawberries with the sugar. Set aside, covered, at room temperature.

For the shortcakes, mix together the flour, sugar, baking powder, baking soda, and salt in the bowl of a food processor. Add the butter pieces and process 15–20 seconds until the butter pieces are pea-sized or smaller. Transfer to a medium bowl. (You can skip the food processor and cut in the butter by hand or with a pastry blender.) Add the buttermilk and mix until just blended. Drop large, heaping tablespoonfuls of the batter in mounds onto the prepared pans at least 2 inches apart.

Bake for 10–12 minutes until the tops start to brown. Remove from the oven and let cool.

When ready to serve, whip the cream with the confectioner's sugar and a dash of vanilla with an electric mixer on medium for a few minutes, just until smooth and mounding. To assemble, split the shortcakes in half horizontally. Over the bottom half, spoon lots of strawberries and their juices as well as a generous dollop of whipped cream. Place the top half of the shortcake on top, a bit askew. Pass remaining strawberries and whipped cream at the table. While best served fresh, leftover components can be stored individually, covered, in the refrigerator for 1–2 days.

Rhubarb Ginger Crumb Cake

Rhubarb isn't just for pie—it makes a fantastic cake, too. Here, I smother diced rhubarb in a buttery batter, then top it off with a crumbly streusel topping studded with crystallized ginger. The result is a beautiful and delicious cake, attractive even to children. Yogurt in the batter makes for a tender crumb. If you don't have crystallized ginger, you can substitute peeled, finely chopped fresh gingerroot, but go easy (start with 1 teaspoon and taste). This cake also makes an excellent breakfast with a dollop of Greek yogurt.

SERVES 8–12

For the cake:

1 cup all-purpose flour

1 teaspoon baking powder

Pinch of salt

1 stick (½ cup) unsalted butter, at cool room temperature

1 cup granulated sugar

2 large eggs, at room temperature

1 teaspoon vanilla extract

⅓ cup plain yogurt

½ pound diced rhubarb, cut into ½-inch pieces (about 2 cups), divided

Preheat the oven to 350°F. Grease and line a 9-inch spring-form pan or standard 9-inch round cake pan with parchment paper.

For the cake, whisk together the flour, baking powder, and salt in a medium bowl. Set aside.

In the bowl of an electric mixer (preferably fitted with a paddle attachment), cream together the butter and sugar on medium speed until fluffy, about 2 minutes. Scraping down the sides and bottom of the bowl as needed, mix in the eggs, one at a time, followed by the vanilla extract. Add half the flour mixture, and blend on low speed briefly. Mix in the yogurt. Reserve 2 tablespoons of the flour mixture and add the rest to the mixer bowl, blending just until combined.

Toss the reserved 2 tablespoons flour mixture with ⅔ of the rhubarb and stir into the batter until combined. Spread the batter in the prepared pan. Scatter the remaining rhubarb on top in a single layer.

For the crumb:

⅓ cup all-purpose flour

⅓ cup light brown sugar, firmly packed

Pinch of salt

2 tablespoons finely chopped crystallized ginger

2 tablespoons cold unsalted butter

For the crumb, combine the flour, brown sugar, and salt in a bowl. Add the chopped crystallized ginger (if you find it too sticky to chop finely, mix in a few pinches of flour). Work the butter into the dry ingredients with your fingers, rubbing the mixture together until the butter incorporates and binds the mixture into small clumps. Shake the bowl so the bigger crumbs rise to the top and sprinkle those over the cake. For the rest, you can either keep working the butter into the mixture to form more clumps or gently squeeze a handful at a time so it binds, then crumble that over the cake.

Bake 45–50 minutes, or until the top is golden brown and a toothpick inserted into the center comes out clean. Let cool. Use a sharp paring knife to loosen the edges of the cake from the pan before unbuckling and removing the ring. Slice and serve with whipped cream. Cake can be stored, covered, at room temperature for 3–4 days.

Cornmeal Lime Sugar Cookies

Cornmeal is a traditional New England ingredient ground from native maize. It's often used to make Yankee corn bread and Rhode Island johnnycakes (a type of hearty pancake). Here, cornmeal adds wholesome flavor and a pleasantly gritty texture to traditional sugar cookies, while a burst of lime brings brightness and acidity. They remind me of the popular sugar cane lime cookies made by Dancing Deer Bakery in Boston.

MAKES ABOUT 3 DOZEN COOKIES

- 1½ cups granulated sugar, plus ½ cup for rolling cookies
- Zest of 1 large lime (about ½ teaspoon), shiny green part only, finely grated with a microplane zester
- 2 sticks (1 cup) unsalted butter, at cool room temperature
- 2½ cups all-purpose flour
- ⅓ cup fine cornmeal
- 1 teaspoon baking soda
- ½ teaspoon baking powder
- ½ teaspoon salt
- 1 large egg
- ½ teaspoon vanilla extract
- Juice of 1 large lime, freshly squeezed (2–3 tablespoons)

Preheat the oven to 350°F. Grease or line two cookie sheets with parchment paper.

With an electric mixer (preferably fitted with a paddle attachment), mix the sugar and lime zest together on low speed until fragrant, about 1 minute. Add the butter and beat, starting on low speed and eventually increasing to medium-high, until fluffy, 2–3 minutes.

Meanwhile, whisk together the flour, cornmeal, baking soda, baking powder, and salt in a medium bowl. Set aside.

Scrape down the sides of the mixer bowl, then add the egg and vanilla extract to the butter mixture. Mix well to combine. Turn off the machine and add half the dry ingredients, then the lime juice, then the rest of the dry ingredients, mixing well and scraping down the bottom and sides of the bowl after each addition. Mix only as long as it takes for the dry ingredients to incorporate and bind into clumps of dough. With your hands, form the dough into balls about 1¼ inches in diameter. Roll in the reserved sugar and place on the prepared pans about 2 inches apart.

Bake 9–11 minutes, just until the edges are set and the tops puff and form hairline cracks, but before the cookies take on any color (ovens vary, so you may want to rotate your pans halfway through for more even cooking). The cookies may seem underbaked, but fear not, they will cool to perfection (soft but not doughy). Remove from the oven and let them sit on the cookie sheets for two minutes before transferring to wire racks. Cooled cookies can be stored in an airtight container for 4–5 days.

Strawberry Rosewater Sorbet

Strawberries start to explode in my area right around the time I notice how beautiful everyone else's rosebushes are (mine died a long time ago). In fact, strawberries and roses are closely related botanically. Rosewater, made by literally soaking rose petals in water, is an ancient flavoring that's very popular in the Middle East. It's sometimes used in pastries found in the Armenian bakeries of Watertown and Belmont, Massachusetts (the area has the third largest Armenian population in the country). This sorbet combines strawberries and rosewater into a simple but elegant flavor. Rosewater gets overpowering really quickly, so I've opted for restraint here, adding just enough to give the strawberry flavor an intriguing boost. If you can't find it, you can make your own rosewater (preferably using homegrown, unsprayed roses) or leave it out. For best results, start the day before you want to serve it to allow enough time to make the base, churn it, and freeze.

MAKES ABOUT 1 QUART

1½ pounds strawberries, hulled

1 cup granulated sugar

1½ tablespoons lemon juice, freshly squeezed

Dash of salt

½–1 tablespoon rosewater

Slice the strawberries and toss them with the sugar, lemon juice, and salt in a large bowl. Let macerate at room temperature for 1 hour (you can stir them once or twice if you think of it).

In a food processor or blender, puree the strawberries with ½ tablespoon rosewater until liquified, about 1 minute. Taste and add another ½ tablespoon rosewater if you want a stronger floral flavor. If desired, strain out the seeds with a fine-mesh strainer (I like to keep them in for texture).

Pour the mixture into an ice cream machine and process according to the manufacturer's instructions. Transfer to a container and freeze at least 6–8 hours. (If you don't have an ice cream machine, see the food processor hack on page 191.) If the sorbet freezes too hard, let the container sit out at room temperature for 5 minutes to soften a bit before serving.

Little Rhubarb Pavlovas

Here's another example of rhubarb playing nicely without a strawberry in sight. The tartness of the braised rhubarb is a perfect contrast to the marshmallowy sweetness of these mini pavlovas, a dessert I'm borrowing from the Australians who invented it. Separate each egg white over a small bowl before adding to the mixing bowl so you don't contaminate the whole batch if you happen to break a yolk. Any fat introduced by a broken yolk will interfere with the whipping process. Save your egg yolks in the fridge covered with a little cold water for a day or two to use for homemade ice cream.

SERVES 10

For the meringues:

4 large egg whites

Pinch of salt

1 cup granulated sugar

2 teaspoons cornstarch

1 teaspoon white wine vinegar (or plain white vinegar)

For the filling:

2 pounds rhubarb, cut into ¾-inch pieces

¾ cup granulated sugar

1 teaspoon vanilla extract

⅛ teaspoon ground cardamom

Pinch of salt

For the whipped cream:

1½ cups cold heavy cream

1 tablespoon confectioner's sugar

Splash of vanilla extract

Preheat the oven to 250°F. Line two sheet pans with parchment paper and trace 10 4-inch circles in pencil using a glass as a guide. Flip the parchment paper over so you can still see the circles.

Separate the yolks from the egg whites gently with clean hands so the yolks don't break. Using an electric mixer, whip the egg whites with the salt in a large bowl on medium-high speed until soft peaks form (when you lift up the beater, the whipped whites form a peak that droops just a little at the tip).

Begin adding the sugar 1 tablespoon at a time with the mixer running. Continue beating on medium-high speed until the mixture is dense, and stiff, glossy peaks form, about 5 minutes. (Rub some meringue on your fingers to make sure all the sugar has dissolved. It should feel smooth, not gritty.) Using a spatula, lightly but thoroughly fold in the cornstarch and vinegar.

Gently spoon the fluffy mixture in the marked circles on the parchment paper, making a well in the middle of each. If the parchment is sliding around too much, use a dab or two of the mixture to glue the paper to the pan.

Bake the pavlovas in the preheated oven for 40–45 minutes until they feel firm on the outside but still soft in the middle. If they crack slightly, that's okay. Then turn off the heat and let them sit inside the oven with the door propped open with a wooden spoon for 20–30 minutes. They should still feel soft in the middle when gently pressed. Remove from the oven and let cool completely.

Increase the oven temperature to 325°F. In a large roasting pan, toss the rhubarb with the sugar, vanilla, cardamom, and salt. Let sit for 20 minutes to draw out some moisture. Then cover tightly with foil and bake for 25–30 minutes until the rhubarb is soft but still holds its shape. Remove from the oven.

Strain the rhubarb in a sieve set over a medium saucepan to catch the juices (don't press or mash—you want the rhubarb to retain its shape). Gently transfer the rhubarb to a medium bowl. Over medium heat, bring the rhubarb juices to a simmer and then reduce for 5 or 6 minutes until syrupy. Pour the syrup over the rhubarb and let cool, then cover and refrigerate until ready to serve.

Assemble the pavlovas just before serving. Whip the cream in a clean bowl with confectioner's sugar and a splash of vanilla until soft, smooth peaks form. Spoon the rhubarb into the wells of the cooled pavlovas and top with softly whipped cream.

Assembled pavlovas should be eaten right away, as they don't keep well. The individual components can be made up to a day ahead of time and stored in airtight containers, the pavlovas at room temperature, and the fruit and whipped cream in the refrigerator for 1–2 days.

Salted Caramel Chocolate Chip Cookie Skillet

The chocolate chip cookie was invented in 1938 at the Toll House Inn in Whitman, Massachusetts, by co-owner Ruth Graves Wakefield and her cook Sue Brides. At that time, chocolate was typically melted before it was mixed into baked goods. But Wakefield had the idea to cut a chocolate bar into little chunks and add those to the cookie dough instead, creating little pockets of chocolate throughout. Thus, a phenomenon was born. This skillet version, adapted from the original Toll House Cookie recipe, improvises further by adding little pools of salted caramel. It's best served warm, slightly underbaked, and topped with Connecticut Valley Vanilla Ice Cream or Maine Buttermilk and Sea Salt Ice Cream.

SERVES 12

2¼ cups all-purpose flour

1 teaspoon baking soda

1 teaspoon salt

2 sticks (1 cup) unsalted butter, at cool room temperature

1 cup light brown sugar, firmly packed

½ cup granulated sugar

2 large eggs, at room temperature

1 teaspoon vanilla

1½ cups bittersweet chocolate chips

1 cup walnut halves

2½ ounces soft caramel candies, like Werther's

Sea salt

Preheat the oven to 350°F. Grease a 10-inch cast iron skillet with butter.

In a medium bowl, whisk together the flour, baking soda, and salt. Set aside.

With an electric mixer (preferably fitted with a paddle attachment), beat the butter, brown sugar, and granulated sugar in a large bowl on medium speed until creamy, about 2 minutes. Add the eggs one at a time, beating well after each addition. Mix in the vanilla. Add the dry ingredients to the butter mixture and mix on low just until combined. On low or by hand, mix in the chocolate chips and nuts.

Scrape the dough into the greased skillet. With a stiff metal spoon, push the dough to the sides of the pan and create some wells in spots for the caramel. Press the caramels into the dough (if they seem too big, you can twist them in half).

Place the skillet in the oven and bake 30–35 minutes until the edges are golden and the center is just set when gently pressed. Remove from the oven and sprinkle top with sea salt while still warm. Let sit 20 minutes in the pan before serving. Cut into wedges and serve with ice cream.

Grape-Nuts Pudding

This mainstay of diners and truck stops across New England is a nostalgic favorite. It contains neither grapes nor nuts, but instead handfuls of Grape-Nuts cereal made from wheat and barley. The little nuggets resemble tiny grape seeds and have a nutty, malted flavor that is also delicious in ice cream (page 212). This pudding doesn't look particularly appealing at first glance—egg custard studded with suspiciously wholesome grains—but it's a delightful treat for young and old, not too sweet, and incredibly easy to make. Don't be put off by the water bath—it's just water in a pan—but it keeps your custard from scorching and preserves the smooth, creamy texture.

SERVES 6–9

3 cups milk (not skim), divided

¾ cup Grape-Nuts cereal

3 large eggs

⅓ cup granulated sugar

3 tablespoons maple syrup

2 teaspoons vanilla extract

½ teaspoon salt

Nutmeg, for sprinkling (preferably freshly grated)

Preheat the oven to 325°F. Grease an 8 × 8-inch baking dish. Set it in a larger roasting pan and fill the gap between the two pans with hot tap water halfway up the sides of the baking dish.

Heat 2 cups of the milk to a bare simmer in a small saucepan. Remove from the heat and stir in the Grape-Nuts. Let soak for 10 minutes while you prepare the other ingredients.

In a large mixing bowl, whisk the eggs together. Add the sugar, maple syrup, vanilla, and salt. Whisk well. Stir in the remaining 1 cup cold milk, followed by the warm Grape-Nuts mixture. Pour into the prepared baking dish. Carefully set the whole water bath apparatus in the oven on the middle shelf.

Bake for about 1 hour, stirring once halfway through the baking time and again 15 minutes later to distribute the Grape-Nuts so they don't all sink to the bottom (unless you prefer it that way, as some do). The custard should be set in the middle (not liquidy) and spring back when gently pressed. Remove from the oven and sprinkle with nutmeg to taste. Let cool 20 minutes. Serve warm or at room temperature with lightly sweetened whipped cream dusted with nutmeg or Connecticut Valley Vanilla Ice Cream. Store, covered, in the refrigerator 3–4 days.

Strawberry Rhubarb Sauce

This is a great recipe to have in your back pocket when you don't have the time or patience for a whole pie, but you want to make use of small batches of strawberries and rhubarb, perhaps from your own garden. It's perfect layered between sponge cake and whipped mascarpone, like the one on page 48, or on a pavlova under a pile of whipped cream and fresh berries. You can spoon it atop Connecticut Valley Vanilla Ice Cream (page 193) or Maine Buttermilk and Sea Salt Ice Cream (page 204) and garnish it with Pie Crisps (page 78). Or layer it with Tapioca Pudding (page 169) in little mason jars for fun throwback parfaits.

SERVES 6–8

- 8 ounces strawberries, hulled, quartered
- 8 ounces rhubarb, stalks cut into ½-inch pieces
- ⅓ cup granulated sugar
- ½ teaspoon vanilla extract
- ½ teaspoon lemon juice, freshly squeezed

Combine all the ingredients in a medium pot over medium heat. Bring to a simmer, lower the heat, and continue to cook 5–15 minutes until saucy (most of the rhubarb will break down while the strawberry pieces remain mostly intact). Let cool. Store in a covered jar in the refrigerator for up to 1 week. If too thick when chilled, you can thin it out with a little water, a teaspoon at a time, until it reaches your desired consistency.

Summer

*N*ew England summers are intoxicating—they'll either fill you with free-spirited euphoria or leave you slumped in a sweaty stupor. On the best days, the picture-perfect combination of sunshine, sparkling water, and lush, green landscapes is a recipe for relaxation and recreation in equal measure. It's a time of warmth and abundance. There's a stretching out of the days and body. We shed our spring jackets and rain boots, trading them in for short sleeves and sandals (or bare feet). We tend our gardens. I feel a general sense of adventure, a wanderlust to explore field and forest, to follow the road less traveled or claim a secret cove for a solitary swim. Just as often, though, I like to stay put and lounge in the fresh air with a good book, sand between my toes, salty breezes in my hair.

One of my favorite summer rituals is riding my bike along the Charles River to the farmers' market on Saturday mornings. Depending on the week, I might find late-season strawberries; plump highbush and tiny lowbush blueberries; ruby red and champagne-colored golden raspberries; dark, shiny blackberries; and perhaps, if I'm lucky, some gooseberries or currants. I'm always a sucker for sweet and sour cherries, juicy peaches and nectarines, and the candy-colored assortment of plums on offer. When the temperatures soar, you can count on ripe melons to follow, from sweet orange muskmelons to refreshing honeydew to red- or yellow-fleshed watermelons, both big and adorably small. U-pick orchards and berry farms abound all over New England, not to mention what you might find walking through the woods or paddling along a pond's edge. I'm always on the lookout for mulberry trees, huckleberry bushes, and black raspberry brambles wherever I go.

All of this gorgeous fruit spells fun in the kitchen. While I eat my fair share fresh and out of hand, I'm also thinking ahead to dessert, like Maine Wild Blueberry Pie (page 45), Plum Cardamom Crisp (page 50), and Peach Raspberry Cornmeal Crumble (page 67). But, let's face it, sometimes it's too hot to even think about turning on the oven. For those days (weeks), there's seasonal homemade ice cream, like Black Raspberry (page 63) and Peach Amaretti (page 55), which is every bit as good as those fluffy, ruffled scoops served up at roadside farm stands and beach-battered clam shacks. Watermelon Lemonade Italian Ice (page 77) and Cantaloupe Creamsicle Ice Cream (page 72) conjure up sweet childhood nostalgia, while Honeydew Jalapeño Ice Pops (page 68) offer a spicy Latin twist on summertime refreshment.

Whether you spend your vacations in the mountains, on the coast, poolside, or in your own backyard, there's a special dessert idea to celebrate every precious week of this fleeting season.

Berries

Strawberries mark the beginning of berry season, but a steady parade of colorful berries follow, all the way through to the fall. Black raspberries, native to New England, start in early summer. Plump highbush blueberries follow in profusion, though you'll have to compete with the birds (and in some places, bears) for your share. Tiny lowbush blueberries (and huckleberries), native to much of New England, are especially abundant in Maine. Red and golden raspberries add a welcome tartness to our summer repertoire (look for them again in the fall, when they make a second appearance). In some areas, you'll also find gooseberries (which look like funny, slightly fuzzy grapes) and tiny bunches of red or white currants. Blackberries come around in late summer. They differ from black raspberries both in their season and flavor. The easiest way to tell them apart is that black raspberries are hollow (like other varieties of raspberries) and blackberries aren't. Choose berries that are bright and shiny, not shriveled. Eat or bake with them as soon as possible, as they lose their luster quickly. Store in the refrigerator to extend their life a few days. For worn-looking fruits slightly past their prime, turn them into sauces, jams, and conserves for ice cream.

Stone Fruits

The term "stone fruit" refers to the pits in the centers of cherries, peaches, nectarines, plums, and their other close relatives. Sweet cherries generally ripen first, including deep burgundy Bing cherries and yellow- and red-blushed Rainier. Smaller, juicier tart cherries (also called sour cherries) follow shortly thereafter, including cherry-red Montmorency. Store cherries in the refrigerator and use them as soon as possible. Fuzzy peaches and their smooth-skinned siblings, nectarines, are like summer sunshine reborn. Pick fruits that are heavy for their size to ensure optimum juiciness, then store them at room temperature until a gentle squeeze yields some give. Plums are too often overshadowed by peaches, but the red-, yellow-, and purple-fleshed varieties all offer beautiful flavor and color to the summer and early fall palate. For dessert preparations, avoid soft, squishy plums that are essentially 100% water. Instead opt for firmer ones (but not rock hard) so they'll hold their shape when baked. You can store plums in the refrigerator to slow down the ripening process.

Melons

Though melons are available at the supermarket year-round, you'll be hard-pressed to find ones as sweet and flavorful as those grown at a local farm. But wherever you find them, do your best to pick a ripe specimen—then plan to use it as soon as possible. All melons should feel heavy for their size. Cantaloupes and orange-fleshed muskmelons go from unripe green to ripe yellow behind the raised beige webbing on their rinds. Smooth-skinned honeydews turn from green to white to yellowish as they ripen. Ideally, they should smell sweet and fragrant, and give a little when you press on the blossom end (that's the end opposite the stem—if you're not sure, try both!). Store them at room temperature to continue ripening or store them in the refrigerator to stall the ripening process. Watermelons are picked ripe, which removes a lot of the guesswork for the consumer, but a yellow field spot (the place where the melon was resting on the ground) tends to indicate a flavorful melon. A thump with your thumb should make a satisfying hollow drum sound. If you're trying to decide between two watermelons, go for the one with the lower-pitched sound.

Maine Wild Blueberry Pie

Wild blueberry pie is the state dessert of Maine, and for good reason. Little lowbush blueberries grow wild in especially large numbers all across the state, thriving in the acidic, glacial soil and cold climate. If you don't have access to these tiny, flavorful blueberries, you can substitute larger cultivated highbush blueberries. Or better yet, buy flash-frozen wild blueberries, like Wyman's. If using frozen, be sure to thaw the berries and drain most of the juices. Mainers prefer their blueberry pies slightly runny, but if you prefer a firmer filling, add an extra tablespoon or two of flour. I've kept this pie pretty traditional, but I couldn't resist adding buttermilk to the crust (Kate's Homemade Butter, which also sells buttermilk, is located in Maine) for extra tenderness and a buttery tang.

SERVES 8–12

For the crust:

2 cups all-purpose flour

1 tablespoon granulated sugar

1 teaspoon salt

1½ sticks (¾ cup) unsalted butter, cut into 12 pieces

4–6 tablespoons cold buttermilk, shaken

For the filling:

1½ pounds fresh or frozen wild blueberries (about 4 cups) (thawed and drained if frozen)

¾ cup granulated sugar

3 tablespoons all-purpose flour

1 teaspoon lemon juice, freshly squeezed

Pinch of cinnamon

Preheat the oven to 425°F. Set aside a 9-inch pie plate (not deep-dish).

For the crust, combine the flour, sugar, and salt in the bowl of a food processor. Add the cold butter and process 10–15 seconds, until the butter pieces stop jumping around like popcorn. Stream 4 tablespoons (¼ cup) buttermilk through the feed tube with the machine running for 2–3 seconds. Add 1 or 2 more tablespoons of buttermilk as needed until the mixture just holds together when gently squeezed. (If you don't have a food processor, you can work the butter into the dry ingredients with a stand mixer fitted with a paddle attachment, a pastry blender, or your fingers.)

Gather the dough together, folding it over once or twice to create layers. Form it into two thick disks, one slightly larger than the other, and wrap in waxed paper, plastic wrap, or reusable wraps. Let it rest in the refrigerator for 20–30 minutes while making the filling.

In a large bowl, combine the blueberries, sugar, flour, lemon juice, and cinnamon.

Flour your counter and rolling pin well. Roll out the larger piece of dough about 12 inches in diameter (slightly less than ¼ inch thick). Transfer the dough to the pie plate by loosening it from the counter with a bench scraper or spatula, and

For preparation:

1 tablespoon unsalted butter, cut into small cubes

1 egg, beaten

1 tablespoon water

draping it over the rolling pin. Center the dough in the pie plate, letting the edges overhang. Pour in the filling.

Roll out the smaller dough disk about 10 inches in diameter. Cut it into strips about ¾ inch wide. Weave a loose lattice over the top of the filling, or just lay them out in a lattice pattern. Fold the edges of the pie dough underneath and crimp with a fork.

In a small bowl, whisk the egg with a teaspoon of water. Brush this egg wash over the crust. Dot the filling with cubes of butter.

Bake the pie 15 minutes at 425°F, then reduce the heat to 350°F. Bake 35–45 minutes more until the juices bubble and the crust is golden brown. (You can cover the crust with foil if needed to prevent it from browning too much.) Remove the pie from the oven and let cool. Pie is best served the day it's made, but leftovers can be stored covered in the refrigerator for 2–3 days.

Raspberry Mascarpone Layer Cake

Why should strawberries have all the fun when it comes to layering with cake and cream? Here tart summer raspberries steal the spotlight, with buttery sponge cake, fresh raspberry jam, and cloudlike layers of whipped mascarpone. Make the jam a day or two before you want to serve the cake to streamline the process (or you can sub in store-bought or farmers' market jam). It should also be noted that this cake is stellar filled with Strawberry Rhubarb Sauce (page 39) and topped with fresh strawberries.

SERVES 8–12

For the filling:

8 ounces raspberries

1 teaspoon lemon juice, freshly squeezed

1 cup granulated sugar, divided

3 tablespoons powdered pectin

For the cake:

4 large eggs

2 cups granulated sugar

2 cups all-purpose flour

2 teaspoons baking powder

½ teaspoon salt

1 cup milk

1 stick unsalted butter, melted

2 teaspoons vanilla extract

For the raspberry filling, mash the raspberries, lemon juice, and 1 tablespoon of the sugar in a small saucepan over medium heat. Cook 2–3 minutes until the raspberries release their juices and come to a hard boil. Add the rest of the sugar and pectin all at once and stir well. Bring back to a hard boil and cook for 1 minute. Remove from the heat and pour through a strainer into a medium bowl to catch the seeds (I like to add a spoonful of seeds back into the jam for a little texture). Let cool to room temperature, then chill in the refrigerator at least 6 hours or overnight. (The jam can be stored in a jar in the fridge for up to 1 month.)

Preheat the oven to 350°F. Grease two 8- or 9-inch pans and line them with parchment paper circles.

For the cake, whip the eggs and sugar in a large bowl with an electric mixer for 5–6 minutes on medium-high speed until thickened and light-colored. In a medium bowl, whisk together the flour, baking powder, and salt. In a small pot or in the microwave, heat the milk to steaming.

Gradually add the dry ingredients to the egg mixture with the mixer on low speed. Gradually add the hot milk, melted butter, and vanilla, and mix on low until combined. Divide the batter between the two prepared pans.

Bake 25–30 minutes until a toothpick inserted into the center comes out with only moist crumbs (no raw batter). Let cool completely before assembling. This cake can be made up to 2 days ahead of time (wrap it in plastic, set back in the cake pan, and refrigerate).

For the whipped mascarpone:

1 (8-ounce) container mascarpone

¼ cup granulated sugar

1 cup heavy cream

For the garnish:

Fresh raspberries

For the frosting, add the mascarpone and sugar to the bowl of an electric mixer. Gradually add the cream and mix on low speed for 1 minute to incorporate the cream and dissolve the sugar. Increase the speed to medium for 1–2 minutes until billowy and able to hold its shape. (Don't take it too far—keep it nice and smooth. If it starts to look rough and spackly, fold in a little bit of cream with a spatula to smooth it out.)

To assemble, layer one cake upside-down on a serving plate (remove the parchment paper). Spread half of the whipped mascarpone almost to the edge. Spoon the raspberry jam on top of the mascarpone. Gently place the second cake upside-down on top. Spread the remaining mascarpone over the cake (frosting the sides is optional). Top with fresh raspberries. Keep refrigerated until ready to serve. Cake will keep covered in the refrigerator for 3–4 days.

Plum Cardamom Crisp

Save your soft, ripe, super-juicy plums for eating out of hand. This recipe is for firmer, slightly underripe plums (or ones that never seem to soften no matter how long they sit out). These will retain some texture after cooking instead of turning into soup. (If you do use very ripe plums, increase the flour to ¼ cup and decrease the sugar to ½ cup.) The color of the finished dessert will depend on what type of plum you're using and whether or not you peel them. For example, yellow-fleshed plums cooked in their purple skins will turn a gorgeous shade of vermillion. Feel free to use any plums you like, or a mix.

SERVES 6–8

For the filling:

2 pounds sliced fresh plums (about 8 medium plums or 12 small), unpeeled

¾ cup granulated sugar

3 tablespoons all-purpose flour

1 teaspoon lemon juice, freshly squeezed

1 teaspoon vanilla extract

½ teaspoon ground cinnamon

½ teaspoon ground cardamom

For the topping:

¾ cup all-purpose flour

½ cup light brown sugar, firmly packed

¼ teaspoon salt

4 tablespoons cold unsalted butter, cut into 4 pieces

⅓ cup chopped walnuts

Preheat the oven to 350°F. Butter the inside of an 8 × 8-inch baking dish or 9-inch pie plate.

For the filling, slice the plums into ½-inch-thick wedges, removing the pits. Combine the plums, sugar, flour, lemon juice, vanilla, and spices in the prepared dish. Set aside.

For the topping, combine the flour, brown sugar, and salt in the bowl of a food processor or an electric mixer. Process briefly to combine. Add the butter. Mix until the butter fully incorporates and the mixture turns crumbly. Add the nuts and pulse a few more times to distribute. (You can also make the topping by hand, cutting the butter into the dry ingredients with your hands or a pastry blender.)

Scatter the mixture over the plums and bake 35–40 minutes, or until the top is golden brown and the juices are bubbly. Remove from the oven and let it cool slightly. Serve warm with Connecticut Valley Vanilla Ice Cream or Maine Buttermilk and Sea Salt Ice Cream.

Summer Fruit Pavlova
with Lemony Whipped Yogurt

The pavlova, a sweet pillow of meringue, was invented in Australia, another British colonial outpost. It was created in homage to the beautiful Russian ballerina, Anna Pavlova. While it's certainly not a traditional New England dessert, it happens to adapt beautifully to local New England fruit. Here, the lemony whipped yogurt creates a deliciously tart contrast with the sweet meringue. (Or, if that's not your thing, you could thin out some of your favorite farmers' market jam and top with unsweetened whipped cream.) Pile high with whatever eye-catching summer fruit you can get your hands on. Don't skimp. Then plan to eat this pavlova all in one sitting, as it does not keep well for any significant length of time. It's very important that you separate your eggs cleanly, with no broken yolks mixed in with the whites. Any fat will interfere with the whipping process. Also, as my Australian recipe-tester taught me—never open the oven door while baking a pavlova. If it should fail to rise (as it sometimes does on a humid day), that's when you put all the components into mason jars and call them parfaits.

For the pavlova:

4 egg whites

⅛ teaspoon salt

1 cup granulated sugar

1½ teaspoons cornstarch

1 teaspoon white vinegar

For the whipped yogurt:

1 cup thick Greek yogurt
(I like Cabot whole milk)

½ cup confectioner's sugar,
sifted

3 tablespoons lemon juice
freshly squeezed

½ teaspoon vanilla extract

Pinch of salt

1 cup heavy cream

For serving:

1 mixed quart of
strawberries, raspberries,
black raspberries,
blueberries, blackberries,
or currants

Preheat oven to 250°F. Line a sheet pan with parchment paper and trace an 8-inch circle on it in pencil using a cake pan or bowl as a guide. Flip the parchment paper over (you should still be able to see the circle).

Using an electric mixer, whip the egg whites with the salt on medium-high speed in a large, clean bowl. When firm peaks form, begin sprinkling in the sugar very slowly, 1 table-spoon at a time, with the mixer running. Once all the sugar is added, continue beating on medium-high speed until stiff, glossy peaks form, 5–8 minutes. Rub some meringue on your fingers to make sure all the sugar has dissolved. Lightly but thoroughly fold in the cornstarch and vinegar.

Gently mound the meringue in the center of the parchment and lightly spread it to fill the circle you traced. With the back of a spoon, shape it so that it's higher on the sides and dipped like a well in the middle. Don't fuss with it too much, though, or you'll lose air. It's meant to look free-form. Bake the pavlova on the middle rack of the preheated oven for 1 hour and 15 minutes, until it's just starting to take on some color and crack slightly (don't open the oven door—turn on the oven light and peek through the window). Then turn off the heat, keeping the oven door closed, and let the meringue cool inside the oven for 1 hour. Remove from the oven and continue to cool undisturbed until ready to serve.

For the topping, combine the Greek yogurt, confectioner's sugar, lemon juice, vanilla, and salt in a medium bowl. With an electric mixer, whip the cream until it holds firm peaks when the beaters are lifted, 1–2 minutes. Scrape the whipped cream on top of the yogurt mixture, and gently fold together with a rubber spatula until combined. The mixture should hold its shape without being too runny. Chill, covered, in the refrigerator until ready to serve.

Assemble just before serving. Spoon the whipped yogurt into the well in the center of the pavlova. Mound the fruit on top. Serve immediately.

Peach Amaretti Ice Cream

Like strawberries, juicy peaches are one of those fruits that just beg to be paired with fresh cream. Choose the ripest summer peaches you can find, preferably from a local orchard, though frozen peaches can be substituted in a pinch. I don't bother to peel the peaches—the skins can be strained out later or sometimes I'll leave them in to create pretty little flecks. Crushed amaretti cookies add texture and boost the flavor of this delicious seasonal ice cream, but you can also leave them out if you wish (or sub in gingersnaps). For best results, start making this ice cream the day before you want to serve it to allow enough time to make the base, churn it, and freeze. For tips on making homemade ice cream, see page 189.

MAKES ABOUT 1½ QUARTS

1 pound peaches (about 3 medium), fuzz rubbed off under water

1 teaspoon lemon juice, freshly squeezed

Pinch of salt

2 large egg yolks

1½ cups heavy cream

1 cup granulated sugar

½ cup crème fraîche (sour cream can be substituted)

½ cup crushed amaretti cookies

Cut the peaches in half and remove the pits. Cut the peach halves into chunks. With a food processor or blender, puree the peaches with the lemon juice and salt until smooth. If using a blender, you can add a little cream if needed to keep things moving.

In a medium saucepan off heat, whisk the yolks, then slowly whisk in the cream. Whisk in the sugar. Cook over medium heat, stirring constantly with a wooden spoon, until it comes to a bare simmer and the mixture develops body, 5–10 minutes. Remove from the heat.

Set a standard mesh strainer in a large bowl. Pour the hot mixture through the strainer into the bowl. To remove the peach skins, pour the peach puree through the strainer. Otherwise, remove the strainer and add the peach puree directly to the cream mixture. Whisk in the crème fraîche. Chill, covered, in the refrigerator until cold, 4–6 hours or overnight.

Freeze in an ice cream maker according to the manufacturer's instructions. Meanwhile, crush the amaretti cookies into crumbs by placing them in a zip-top bag and smashing them with a can or meat mallet. As you spoon the ice cream into a freezer-safe container, alternate with thin layers of amaretti crumbs. Freeze until firm, 6–8 hours.

Note: For instructions on how to make ice cream without a machine, see page 190.

Sweet Cherry Black Raspberry Cobbler

Black raspberries add a burst of tartness to the sweet cherries in this beautiful rustic cobbler. If you can't find black raspberries, you can substitute sour cherries (if you can find them), blackberries, or just add an extra cup of sweet cherries plus a heavy hand with the lemon juice. There's no need for a cherry pitter for this recipe since the cherries are halved, Just tear the cherries in half at the stem end and pull out the pits with your fingers. (It's best to do this in a bowl over the sink.) If using frozen cherries, defrost them first and drain the juices before adding. When baking, set a rimmed sheet pan on the rack underneath the cobbler to keep any overflowing juices from smoking in the bottom of your oven. If you don't have a heating element at the top of your oven, consider using the broiler for a few minutes to give the biscuits a rich golden-brown color.

SERVES 8–12

For the fruit mix:

5 cups sweet cherries, stemmed, pitted, halved

1 cup black raspberries

½ cup granulated sugar, plus 1 tablespoon for topping

3 tablespoons cornstarch

Juice from ½ small lemon, freshly squeezed (about 1 tablespoon)

1 tablespoon vanilla extract

¼ teaspoon almond extract

Pinch of ground cinnamon

Preheat the oven to 375°F. Butter a 9-inch deep-dish pie plate.

Combine the pitted cherries, black raspberries, sugar, cornstarch, lemon juice, vanilla, almond extract, and cinnamon in a large bowl. Stir well.

Add the flour, baking powder, and salt to the bowl of a food processor, and pulse the motor to combine. Add the butter and pulse until the mixture forms a coarse meal, 15–30 seconds depending on the size of your cubes. Dump the mixture into a medium bowl and add the milk. Mix with a fork until a scrappy dough forms. (If you don't have a food processor, you can cut the butter into the dry ingredients in a mixing bowl with a pastry blender, fork and knife, or your fingers.)

Turn the dough onto the counter and gently knead three or four times, folding the dough over on itself, until it comes together. If the dough seems too dry, drizzle a tiny bit more milk over the dry areas and knead again once or twice. Press the dough into a disk about ½ inch thick. With a 2–3 inch biscuit cutter or jelly jar, cut straight down through the dough into enough circles to cover the cobbler (recombine the

For the biscuits:

2 cups flour

2 teaspoons baking powder

½ teaspoon salt

1½ sticks (¾ cup) cold unsalted butter, cut into small cubes

½ cup milk, plus 1 teaspoon for the topping

scraps to make extra biscuits). Arrange the biscuits on top, brush with a little milk, and sprinkle with the remaining sugar.

Bake uncovered until the fruit is bubbling and the biscuits are golden brown, 45–50 minutes. Let cool at least 10 minutes. Serve with vanilla ice cream or a dollop of crème fraîche. Leftovers can be stored covered in the refrigerator 2–3 days and reheated in the microwave.

Sand Dollar Cookies

My kids grew up spending time on the beaches of Cape Cod Bay, wading in tidal pools and corralling hermit crabs, moon snails, and other marine creatures through elaborate sand structures. Finding a sand dollar was the jackpot. The delicate hollow disks are the exoskeletons of a flat, burrowing sea urchin. These cookies remind me of those breezy summer days. You can make the dough a few days in advance. Keep it tightly wrapped in the refrigerator and let it stand at room temperature for a half hour before rolling out. If you don't have cardamom, you can substitute ½ teaspoon ground cinnamon.

MAKES ABOUT 2 DOZEN

1⅔ cups all-purpose flour

¼ teaspoon baking powder

¼ teaspoon fine sea salt

1 stick (½ cup) unsalted butter, at cool room temperature

1 cup confectioner's sugar, sifted

2 large eggs (one separated)

½ teaspoon vanilla extract

¼ teaspoon almond extract

2 tablespoons granulated sugar

½ teaspoon ground cardamom

Sliced almonds (preferably a full bag so you can pick out the prettiest slices)

In a medium bowl, sift together the flour, baking powder, and salt. Set aside.

With an electric mixer (preferably fitted with a paddle attachment), beat the butter and confectioner's sugar on medium speed until creamy, 1–2 minutes. Add the whole egg, egg yolk, vanilla, and almond extract (reserve the egg white for decoration). Mix until smooth and fluffy, 1–2 minutes.

Add the flour mixture to the butter mixture, and mix at low speed just until incorporated. Shape the dough into a flat disk and wrap it in plastic wrap. Chill in the refrigerator for 2 hours.

Preheat the oven to 350°F. Line cookie sheets with parchment paper.

On a lightly floured counter, roll out the dough ⅛ inch thick. Cut out circles with a 2½-inch biscuit cutter or juice glass. Place the rounds on the prepared pans and brush with lightly beaten egg white. Stir together the granulated sugar and ground cardamom in a small bowl, and sprinkle over the cookies. Gently press 5 almond slices in a star shape in the center of each cookie.

Bake for 4 minutes. Remove the pan from the oven and gently press the almonds into the cookies again. Sprinkle with additional cardamom-sugar if desired. Bake for 8–10 more minutes or until the centers are firm. Remove the cookies to wire racks and let cool completely. Cookies can be stored in an airtight container at room temperature for 4–5 days.

Lemon Blueberry Cake

Blueberry and lemon are such a classic combination, I couldn't pass up the opportunity to speckle a layer cake with wild blueberries and then slather it with a lemony cream cheese frosting. I prefer to use the little wild blueberries in this cake because, if given the choice, I'd rather have more small pops of flavor than fewer big ones. But the bigger, plumper blueberries do make an enticing garnish. That said, use what you have. (I don't recommend using frozen blueberries, however, as they tend to turn the batter gray.) While this is the perfect cake to serve at your summer picnic or garden party, the frosting doesn't stand up well to heat. Keep refrigerated until absolutely ready to serve.

SERVES 12–16

For the cake:

1 teaspoon lemon zest (from 2 medium lemons)

1⅓ cups granulated sugar

1½ sticks (¾ cup) unsalted butter, at cool room temperature

3 large eggs, at room temperature

1 teaspoon vanilla extract

2 cups all-purpose flour, plus 1 tablespoon to dredge the blueberries

1 teaspoon baking powder

½ teaspoon baking soda

¼ teaspoon salt

1 cup buttermilk, shaken

2 cups fresh wild blueberries (about 1 pint)

¼ teaspoon ground cinnamon

Preheat the oven to 350°F. Grease two 8-inch cake pans, then line each with a circle of parchment paper.

Rub the lemon zest into the sugar until moist and fragrant. With an electric mixer (preferably fitted with a paddle attachment), beat the butter on medium-high speed for 1 minute. Scrape down the bottom and sides of the bowl as needed. Add the lemon sugar and continue to beat 2–3 more minutes until very fluffy. Add the eggs one at a time, mixing well after each addition. Then mix in the vanilla.

In a medium bowl, whisk together the flour, baking powder, baking soda, and salt. Gently heat the buttermilk in the microwave just to get the chill out (don't overheat). Add half of the dry ingredients to the butter mixture and mix on low speed until combined. Slowly add the buttermilk with the mixer running on low, scraping down the bottom and sides of the bowl as needed. Then add the rest of the dry ingredients and mix on low.

Toss the washed blueberries with 1 tablespoon of flour and the cinnamon until coated. Gently fold the blueberries into the batter with a rubber spatula. Spread the batter into the prepared pans and bake 30–35 minutes. Let cool completely.

For the frosting:

1 (8-ounce) package cream cheese, at cool room temperature

1 stick (½ cup) unsalted butter, at cool room temperature

3 cups confectioner's sugar, sifted

1 teaspoon lemon zest (from 2 medium lemons)

2 tablespoons freshly squeezed lemon juice

1 teaspoon vanilla extract

Pinch of salt

For the garnish:

Fresh blueberries and lemon zest

For the frosting, beat the cream cheese and butter together with an electric mixer (preferably fitted with a paddle attachment) until very smooth, 2–3 minutes. Add the sifted confectioner's sugar in three batches, starting on low then increasing speed, mixing well after each addition. Add the lemon zest, lemon juice, vanilla, and salt. Mix on medium until combined. (If the frosting is very soft, let it chill in the refrigerator for 20–30 minutes to firm up a bit.)

To assemble the layer cake, remove the individual cakes from the pans by running a knife along the edges and flipping them out onto a plate. Remove the parchment paper. Flip one cake right-side-up onto a serving plate. Spread a layer of frosting across the top. Flip the second cake upside-down on top and center. Frost the sides of the cake, then the top. Decorate with blueberries and lemon zest. The cake can be kept covered in the refrigerator for up to 5 days.

Black Raspberry Ice Cream

You know you're in New England when Black Raspberry Ice Cream is a staple on local ice cream boards. Native to North America, black raspberries are often found growing wild in early to mid-summer along field and forest edges or overgrown, abandoned spaces in a brambly thicket. They're often mistaken for blackberries, but they tend to be smaller and always have a hollow core like other raspberries (blackberries have solid centers and ripen later in the summer). Black raspberries have a unique flavor, sweeter than a blackberry but wilder than their red raspberry cousins. Pick the darkest purple ones, almost black, for the best flavor. If you can't get your hands on them, try this recipe with half red raspberries and half blackberries instead. Because of the number of steps that involve time in the refrigerator and freezer, I recommend starting the process a day or two before you intend to serve it. For tips on making homemade ice cream, see page 189.

MAKES ABOUT 1 QUART

1 pint black raspberries

1 cup granulated sugar, divided

Juice of ½ medium lemon, freshly squeezed (about 1 tablespoon)

2½ cups heavy cream, divided

2 large egg yolks

In a food processor, pulse the black raspberries with ½ cup of the sugar and the lemon juice until you have a chunky puree. Let sit 20–30 minutes to allow the juices to come out.

Meanwhile, add ½ cup of the cream to a large bowl. Set a strainer over the bowl and place near the stove.

In a medium saucepan off heat, whisk the yolks, then slowly whisk in the remaining 2 cups of cream. Whisk in the remaining ½ cup of sugar all at once. Cook over medium heat, stirring constantly with a wooden spoon, until it comes to a bare simmer, 5–8 minutes. Remove from the heat and pour the hot mixture into the strainer bowl.

Run the black raspberry puree through a food mill on its finest setting set over the bowl with the cream. (If you don't have a food mill, you can push the mixture through a fine-meshed sieve with a spatula or wooden spoon.)

Stir the mixture well and chill, covered, in the refrigerator until cold, 4–6 hours or overnight.

Freeze in an ice cream maker according to the manufacturer's instructions. Transfer to a freezer-safe container and freeze until firm, 6–8 hours.

Note: For instructions on how to make ice cream without a machine, see page 190.

Variation

Purple Cow: While the ice cream is churning, measure 2 ounces each of chopped dark chocolate and white chocolate (not chips) in separate small microwaveable bowls. Heat in the microwave, stirring every 30 seconds or so, until melted and smooth, about 1 minute. (If you don't have a microwave, you can improvise a double boiler by putting the dark and white chocolates in separate metal bowls, and alternate setting them on top of a small saucepan with an inch of simmering water, stirring often until melted.) Time it so the chocolate is still warm when the ice cream is finished churning. As you transfer the churned ice cream to a freezer-safe container, alternate drizzling it lightly with the melted dark and white chocolate, stirring vigorously with a fork as you go. The cold ice cream will harden the warm chocolate, and the motion will turn the chocolate into little chips. Freeze until firm, 6–8 hours.

Plum Torte

This torte is a favorite recipe due to its versatility in all seasons. In my previous book, Winter-sweet, *I flavored it with almonds and cranberries. In the spring, I love it with rhubarb. Here, I combine plums and cinnamon. I love using late summer Italian prune plums, but any variety of plum will do. Choose specimens that are firm with a little give; not hard as a rock and not swollen and squishy like water balloons. Arrange the plum wedges in a spiral pattern for a striking presentation, but a rustic, messy approach works too.*

SERVES 12

1 cup all-purpose flour

1 teaspoon baking powder

¼ teaspoon ground cinnamon

Pinch of salt

1 stick (½ cup) unsalted butter, at cool room temperature

1 cup granulated sugar, plus 1 teaspoon for topping

2 large eggs, at room temperature

½ pound ripe but firm plums, stemmed, pitted, each cut into 6 wedges

Preheat the oven to 350°F. Grease or line a 9-inch springform pan with a circle of parchment paper (you can also use a 9-inch standard cake pan).

In a medium bowl, sift together the flour, baking powder, cinnamon, and salt. Set aside.

In the bowl of a stand mixer (preferably fitted with a paddle attachment), cream together the butter and sugar on medium speed until fluffy, 1–2 minutes. Scrape down the sides and bottom of the bowl and mix in the eggs, one at a time. Add the flour mixture, and spin on low speed just until combined.

Spread the batter in the prepared pan (it will be very thick and look like not nearly enough, but it will puff up in the oven). Arrange the plum wedges on top of the batter in a single layer. Sprinkle the remaining 1 teaspoon sugar over the top of the torte.

Bake 40–45 minutes, or until the top is golden brown and a toothpick inserted into the center comes out clean. Let cool. Use a sharp paring knife to loosen the edges of the cake from the pan before unbuckling and removing the ring. Remove the pan bottom and parchment paper by sliding a spatula between the cake and the bottom of the pan. Set the torte on a serving plate and slice. Serve with lightly sweetened whipped cream.

Every Berry Buttermilk Buckle

A buckle is an old-fashioned butter cake, with or without a crumb topping. The name is said to come from the way the cake buckles under the weight of the fruit as the batter rises in the oven. Any seasonal berries will do: raspberries, mulberries, strawberries, blackberries, gooseberries. The world is your orchard. Even stone fruits likes peaches, nectarines, and cherries are fair game. As the berries cook, the fragrant juices infuse the cake with jammy flavor. It's great for dessert or breakfast, with or without a dollop of Greek yogurt.

SERVES 8–12

For the cake:

1 cup all-purpose flour

¼ teaspoon baking soda

¼ teaspoon salt

Pinch of cinnamon

1 stick (½ cup) unsalted butter, at room temperature

1 cup granulated sugar

1 large egg

1 teaspoon vanilla extract

⅓ cup buttermilk

3 cups assorted fresh berries

For the topping:

⅓ cup all-purpose flour

⅓ cup light brown sugar, firmly packed

Pinch of salt

2 tablespoons unsalted butter, melted

Preheat the oven to 350°F. Grease and line a 9-inch spring-form pan or standard cake pan with parchment paper.

In a medium bowl, sift together the flour, baking soda, salt, and cinnamon. Set aside.

With an electric mixer (preferably fitted with a paddle attachment), cream together the butter and sugar on medium speed until fluffy, about 2 minutes. Scraping down the sides and bottom of the bowl as needed, mix in the egg followed by the vanilla extract. Add about ⅔ of the flour mixture, and blend on low speed briefly. Warm the buttermilk slightly in the microwave to reduce the chill, 30–40 seconds (don't overheat). Slowly mix in the buttermilk, then the rest of the dry ingredients, mixing just until combined.

Wash the berries and toss with a few pinches of flour. Gently fold in ⅔ of the berries by hand with a rubber spatula. Spread the batter in the prepared pan. Scatter the remaining berries on top in a single layer.

For the topping, mix the dry ingredients in a small bowl. Stir in the melted butter until crumbly clumps form. Scatter on top of the buckle.

Bake 55–60 minutes, or until the top is golden brown and a toothpick inserted into the center comes out with moist crumbs only, no raw batter. Let cool. Use a sharp paring knife to loosen the edges of the cake from the pan. Turn out onto a plate and unpeel the parchment paper. Serve plain, with whipped cream, or with Greek yogurt. The cake can be stored, covered, at room temperature for 2–3 days (refrigerated, 4–5 days).

Peach Raspberry Cornmeal Crumble

I like to mix summertime fruits in baked desserts, letting tart berries liven up the very sweet stone fruits. Peaches and raspberries are a classic pairing. Their flavors complement each other nicely and they come into season around the same time. I leave the peels on the peaches for color and texture, but you can remove them if you wish. Feel free to sub in nectarines or plums for the peaches, and blackberries for the raspberries as the season progresses. Cornmeal lends a pleasant crunch to the buttery, crumbly topping, and the technique couldn't be easier— just stir in melted butter.

SERVES 6–8

For the filling:

2 pounds ripe peaches, pitted, sliced

1 cup raspberries

½ cup light brown sugar, firmly packed

2 tablespoons all-purpose flour

Juice of ½ lemon, freshly squeezed (about 1 tablespoon)

For the topping:

⅔ cup all-purpose flour

⅓ cup yellow cornmeal

¼ cup light brown sugar, firmly packed

2 tablespoons granulated sugar

½ teaspoon baking powder

¼ teaspoon salt

4 tablespoons unsalted butter, melted

Preheat the oven to 350°F. Butter the inside of a 9-inch deep-dish pie plate.

For the filling, combine the peaches, raspberries, brown sugar, flour, and lemon juice in a large bowl. Pour into the prepared baking dish.

For the topping, whisk the flour, cornmeal, sugars, baking powder, and salt in a medium bowl. Add the melted butter and stir with a wooden spoon until well combined and the mixture forms clumps. Scatter over the top of the fruit.

Bake 45–50 minutes until the fruit is bubbly and the topping is golden brown. Serve with Connecticut Valley Vanilla Ice Cream (page 193) or Maine Buttermilk and Sea Salt Ice Cream (page 204) (or simply a splash of heavy cream).

Honeydew Jalapeño Ice Pops

Popsicles are a ubiquitous childhood summertime treat—but most of them are artificially flavored and unnaturally colored. These refreshing and colorful popsicles burst with fresh, locally grown fruit, yet still feel exciting and exotic. Inspired by Mexican ice pops, they're the perfect way to beat the summer heat. Selecting a ripe melon is no easy feat, but the honey and lime will perk up even a slightly underripe melon. To gauge ripeness, look for honeydews that feel heavy for their size, preferably with a pale yellow cast to the skin. The stem end should give slightly when pressed and smell fresh and slightly sweet. I'm a sucker for contrasting flavors, and these ice pops strike a tantalizing balance between sweet and tart. To add a playful burn to this frozen treat, I've added fresh jalapeño seeds. The more you add, the spicier the pops will be. Just be sure not to touch your eyes while seeding the hot peppers, and wash your hands thoroughly afterwards.

MAKES 8

½ cup water

½ cup granulated sugar

1 tablespoon honey

1 pound (3 cups) peeled, cubed honeydew (about ½ large melon)

Zest of 1 lime (about 1 teaspoon)

1½ tablespoons freshly squeezed lime juice

Pinch of salt

¼ teaspoon jalapeño seeds from 1 fresh jalapeno, sliced lengthwise (optional)

In a small saucepan, combine the water, sugar, and honey over medium-high heat, stirring often until the sugar dissolves and the mixture comes to a boil. Let cool. Puree the melon and the sugar syrup in a blender or food processor. Stir in the lime zest, lime juice, and salt.

Drop the jalapeño seeds into the popsicle molds. Spoon the melon mixture into the molds almost to the top. Cover with the lid and insert popsicle sticks halfway. Freeze until solid, 5–6 hours.

To serve, run hot water over the ice pop molds for several seconds, remove the lid, and gently pull out, taking care not to pull the stick out of the pop itself. Pops can be stored in the freezer in molds or removed, wrapped in waxed paper, and stored in a freezer bag for months.

Brandied Cherries

They say no sundae is complete without a cherry on top, and I agree 100%. But gone are the unnaturally fluorescent maraschino cherries of my youth in favor of these dark and sultry things: fresh cherries lightly sweetened and soaked in brandy. Same fun, different flavor. If you don't have brandy, try whiskey, bourbon, or port. For an alcohol-free version, just sub in water for the brandy. While frozen cherries work well for pies, I don't recommend them here because the texture will be too mushy. The almond extract really boosts the cherry flavor, so I encourage you to use it. Just be sure to label the jar for anyone who might have nut allergies.

MAKES ABOUT 1 PINT

8 ounces fresh sweet
   cherries, stemmed
⅓ cup granulated sugar
2 tablespoons brandy
½ teaspoon freshly
   squeezed lemon juice
¼ teaspoon almond extract

Pit the cherries with a cherry pitter or chopstick pushed through the stem end over a bowl in the sink (try to keep the cherries whole, if you can). Another way is to mash them slightly with the side of a large knife and then pull the pit out (but be warned, this is messy, staining work).

Add the pitted cherries, sugar, brandy, and lemon juice to a small saucepan. Set over medium heat, stirring frequently. Bring to a simmer and reduce the heat to low. Simmer the cherries 3–5 minutes, stirring occasionally, until the cherries soften a bit (but aren't soft) and the liquid turns foamy on top, and syrupy on the bottom. Do not overcook; you want the fruit to retain some of its structure.

Remove from the heat and add the almond extract. Let cool. Transfer the cherries and syrup to a bowl or jar, cover, and chill until cold. Top your ice cream sundaes with the cherries using a slotted spoon, or spoon the cherries and syrup over vanilla ice cream. You can also make a cherry frappe with the leftover syrup and vanilla ice cream (page 205).

Cantaloupe Creamsicle Ice Cream

The approach of the neighborhood ice cream truck, with its jingly ragtime tunes, has been burned into my brain forever. I loved orange Creamsicles for the way the refreshing, citrusy orange sherbet complemented the velvety vanilla ice cream. This homemade version leans on local summer cantaloupe (and other orange muskmelons) rather than oranges for the bulk of its flavor and color. To select a melon, look for one that's heavy for its size, slightly fragrant, and gives slightly when you press on the stem end. Avoid overripe cantaloupes for this recipe, as they can develop some funky flavors with age (taste first). I recommend making this ice cream 1–2 days before you want to eat it. Serve on a hot summer day, perhaps with a sprig of mint, and feel like a kid again.

MAKES ABOUT 1 QUART

- ¾ pound (about 2 cups) ripe cantaloupe, cubed small (about ½ medium melon)
- ¾ cup granulated sugar, divided
- 1 tablespoon freshly squeezed lemon juice
- 1½ cups heavy cream, divided
- ½ cup milk (preferably whole, but not skim)
- 2 teaspoons vanilla extract
- 2 large egg yolks
- Pinch of salt

To peel the cantaloupe, first cut a thin slice off the stem end and the blossom end of the melon. Flip it on to one of those flat ends and then cut ¼-inch deep along the sides, following the curved contour of the melon, to remove the rind in a thick strip. Continue peeling around the perimeter of the melon in this fashion. Flip the cantaloupe over to make sure you didn't miss any rind. Halve the melon lengthwise and scoop out the seeds. Cut the cantaloupe into ¾-inch cubes and measure out what you need.

Add the cubed cantaloupe and 1 tablespoon of the sugar to a small saucepan over medium-low heat. Cook, stirring occasionally, for 3–4 minutes until the melon starts to release its juices (if your melon is dry, you may have to add a little water). Bring to a simmer and cook 8–10 minutes more, stirring occasionally. As cantaloupe softens, mash with a potato masher and cook until the melon has broken down completely. Remove from the heat and let cool.

Puree the cantaloupe mixture together with the lemon juice in a blender or food processor. You should have about 1 cup of cantaloupe puree.

Add ¾ cup of the cream, all the milk, and the vanilla to a large bowl. Set a fine-mesh sieve over the bowl and place near the stove.

In a medium saucepan off heat, whisk the yolks, then slowly whisk in the remaining ¾ cup of cream. Add the remaining sugar and salt, then whisk to dissolve. Cook over medium-low heat, stirring constantly with a wooden spoon, until it comes to a bare simmer, 5–8 minutes. Pour the mixture into the sieve, followed by the cantaloupe puree. Remove the sieve, stir, and let cool. Cover and refrigerate until cold, 4–6 hours or overnight.

Freeze in an ice cream maker according to the manufacturer's instructions, then transfer to a freezer-safe container and freeze until firm, 6–8 hours.

Note: For instructions on how to make ice cream without a machine, see page 190.

Peach Blueberry Tarts

Italian free-form tarts called crostatas are the pastries on which these are based. The advantages are lots of crisp crust, individual portions (if you so choose), and a low-key, non-fussy approach to presentation. Peach and blueberries make lovely bedfellows, but feel free to combine other seasonal fruits such as plums and raspberries. Serve with a scoop of Connecticut Valley Vanilla Ice Cream or Maine Buttermilk and Sea Salt Ice Cream for a stunner of a summer treat.

SERVES 8–12

For the crust:

2 cups all-purpose flour

1 tablespoon granulated sugar

1 teaspoon salt

1½ sticks (¾ cup) cold unsalted butter, cut into 12 pieces

4–6 tablespoons ice water

For the filling:

¼ cup granulated sugar

¼ cup light brown sugar, firmly packed

2 tablespoons all-purpose flour

2 pounds ripe peaches (about 6 or 7 medium), unpeeled, pits removed

1 cup blueberries (about ½ pint)

1 teaspoon freshly squeezed lemon juice

1 teaspoon vanilla extract

Freshly grated nutmeg, to taste

1 large egg, beaten

Preheat the oven to 425°F. Grease or line one rimmed sheet pan with parchment paper.

For the crust, combine the flour, sugar, and salt in the bowl of a food processor. Add the cold butter and process 10–15 seconds, until the butter pieces stop jumping around like popcorn. Add ¼ cup ice water and process 2–3 seconds. If needed, add additional water 1 tablespoon at a time, pulsing the motor 5–6 times to mix. Stop when the dough starts to come together and holds its shape when gently squeezed. (If you don't have a food processor, you can also work the butter into the dry ingredients with a stand mixer fitted with a paddle attachment, a pastry blender, or your fingers.)

Gather the dough together, gently kneading once or twice to make sure it holds together. Cut into 6 more-or-less equal pieces. Form each into a disk and wrap in waxed paper, plastic wrap, or reusable wraps. Let rest in the refrigerator 20–30 minutes while making filling.

For the filling, combine the sugar, brown sugar, and flour in a small bowl and set aside. Slice the peaches no more than ½ inch thick. Combine with the blueberries in a large bowl. Mix in the lemon juice, vanilla, and nutmeg.

Flour your counter and rolling pin well. Roll out one disk of dough to about 7 inches in diameter (slightly less than ¼ inch thick). Transfer the dough to the prepared pan by loosening the dough from the counter a little at a time with a bench scraper or spatula, and draping it over the rolling pin. Spoon ⅙ of the fruit filling in the center of the dough, leaving a 1-inch margin around the edge. Sprinkle about a tablespoon of the sugar mixture over the fruit. Fold over the edges to form a rough circle or whatever shape you like. Brush the crust with beaten egg mixed with a teaspoon of water. Repeat with the remaining disks of dough and filling. Divide any remaining sugar mixture among the tarts.

Bake 15 minutes at 425°F, then reduce the temperature to 375°F and bake 25–30 minutes more, until the crust is golden brown and the filling is bubbly and thick. Let cool at least a half hour so the filling can set. Serve with Connecticut Valley Vanilla Ice Cream or Maine Buttermilk and Sea Salt Ice Cream. These tarts are best eaten the day they're made, but they can be stored covered in the refrigerator for 1–2 days.

Watermelon Lemonade Italian Ice

I remember the old-fashioned Italian ice of my childhood that came in little wax cups with a pull-tab top. It was always a toss-up between watermelon and lemon on a hot day. Here, I've combined both flavors. For a finely textured Italian ice like those little wax cups, use the food processor method below. For a coarser granita, see the instructions that follow.

SERVES 4–6

Zest of 1 lemon (about ½ teaspoon), shiny yellow part only

1 cup granulated sugar

2 pounds peeled, cubed watermelon (about 6 cups)

¼ cup freshly squeezed lemon juice (from 2–3 medium lemons)

In a small bowl, rub the lemon zest into the sugar with your fingers until moist and fragrant.

In a large bowl, toss the watermelon cubes with the lemon sugar, and mash with a potato masher into a chunky soup. Cover and let sit at room temperature for 3 hours.

Pour the watermelon mixture into a mesh strainer over another large bowl, pressing to extract the syrup with a wooden spoon or rubber spatula. You should have about 2½ cups of syrup. If you have significantly less, return the watermelon to the original bowl, mash it some more, and strain it again, adding it to the bowl of syrup. Stir the lemon juice into the watermelon syrup.

Freeze the mixture in a resealable bag laid flat in a metal roasting pan (or pour it right into the roasting pan) until frozen.

Break the ice into small chunks in the bag first and then transfer them to the bowl of a food processor. Process 2–3 minutes, until completely smooth. (You may need to stop the machine occasionally and break up the larger chunks with a spoon. If some chunks are resisting, keep running the machine for up to 5 minutes and the friction should generate just enough heat to soften them up.) Portion into 4–6 ramekins, leaving ¼ inch at the top for expansion as it refreezes. Set the ramekins in a small pan, cover with plastic wrap, and freeze until ready to serve.

For a coarser, more granular texture, freeze in a medium metal bowl for 30 minutes. Stir with a fork, scraping the frozen crystals from the outer edges toward the center. Return to the freezer in 30-minute increments, repeating the process of stirring from the edges toward the center, until it turns from slush to a coarse shaved ice.

Pie Crisps

Everyone loves pie à la mode—fresh fruit pie with a scoop of vanilla ice cream—but I'm turning the ratio upside down, topping a scoop of ice cream with a fresh fruit compote and home-made pie crisps. Use whatever flavor of ice cream you want (vanilla, buttermilk, maple) and use whatever seasonal fruit sauce you like (strawberry rhubarb, blueberry, peach ginger, spiced apple). This is a great place for a novice pie baker to start: spectacular results without outrageous effort. For best results, break the pie crisps into smaller pieces after serving for easier eating.

SERVES 8–10 (OR MORE, DEPENDING ON SIZE)

1 cup all-purpose flour

1 teaspoon granulated sugar, plus more for sprinkling

½ teaspoon salt

6 tablespoons cold, unsalted butter, cut into 6 pieces

3 tablespoons ice water

1 teaspoon milk

In a food processor, pulse the flour, sugar, and salt until combined. Add the cold butter, and run the machine 10–15 seconds. Add the ice water and run the machine 5–10 seconds more, until the dough starts to clump. (If you don't have a food processor, you can also work the butter into the dry ingredients with a stand mixer fitted with a paddle attachment, a pastry blender, or your fingers.)

Dump the mixture onto a sheet of waxed paper, plastic wrap, or reusable wrap. Gather the dough together, handling it as quickly and as little as possible, and form it into a disk. Fold it over onto itself once or twice to create layers, and press it into a disk again. Wrap it up and refrigerate 15–20 minutes while the oven preheats.

Preheat the oven to 375°F. Grease or line a cookie sheet with parchment paper. Flour the counter and rolling pin thoroughly. Gather cookie cutters (rounds, leaves, stars) or a small juice glass to cut the dough into 2- to 3-inch shapes (smaller is better). Alternatively, you can cut the dough with a knife into trapezoidal shapes, keeping them as evenly sized as possible.

Remove the dough from the refrigerator and roll it out ¼-inch thick on the floured counter. Cut out shapes and set them on the prepared pan, leaving a little space between them. Press together the scraps, reroll, and cut until you use all the dough. If the dough is getting soft and difficult to handle, set the whole pan in the refrigerator for 15 minutes before baking.

When ready to bake, brush the cutouts with milk and sprinkle with sugar. Bake 16–20 minutes (or more depending on the size) until deeply golden brown for best flavor. Serve atop ice cream with the fruit sauce of your choice.

Spiced Heirloom Tomato Cake with Sour Cream Frosting

As summer wanes and the first faint whispers of fall make themselves heard through the trees, you may find yourself with an unreasonable number of tomatoes. I realize cake might not be the first thing that jumps to mind for your tomato glut, but why not? This cake is completely delicious, scented with cinnamon and allspice, and the luscious sour cream frosting provides just the right amount of tang. Choose a fresh heirloom tomato because they tend to have a meatier constitution (meaning, more flesh and fewer seeds). Garnish with late summer flowers.

SERVES 12

For the cake:

1½ cups all-purpose flour

1 teaspoon baking powder

½ teaspoon baking soda

½ teaspoon ground cinnamon

¼ teaspoon ground allspice

¼ teaspoon salt

1 stick (½ cup) unsalted butter, at room temperature

1 cup light brown sugar, firmly packed

1 medium heirloom tomato (at least 5 ounces)

2 large eggs, at room temperature

1 teaspoon vanilla extract

Preheat the oven to 350°F. Grease or line a 9-inch springform pan with parchment paper.

In a medium bowl, whisk together the flour, baking powder, baking soda, spices, and salt. Set aside.

With an electric mixer (preferably fitted with a paddle attachment), beat the butter until creamy. Add the brown sugar and mix on medium-high until fluffy, 1–2 minutes.

Meanwhile, grate the tomato on the large holes of a box grater over a shallow bowl. Measure out ⅓ cup tomato pulp. Set aside.

Add the eggs to the butter mixture, one at a time, scraping down the sides and bottom of the bowl and mixing well after each addition. Mix in the vanilla. Add half of the dry ingredients and mix on low speed just until incorporated. Add the tomato pulp and mix gently on low to incorporate. Add the rest of the dry ingredients and mix on low just to combine.

Spread the batter in the prepared pan and bake 30–35 minutes, until the cake is deeply browned and a toothpick inserted into the center comes out clean. Let cool completely.

For the frosting:

1 stick (½ cup) unsalted butter, at room temperature

1½ cups confectioner's sugar, sifted

½ teaspoon vanilla extract

¼ cup sour cream

For the frosting, beat the butter with an electric mixer (again, preferably fitted with a paddle attachment) until smooth and creamy. Add the sifted confectioner's sugar in three batches, scraping down the sides and bottom of the bowl and beating well after each addition. Add the vanilla and mix well. Add the sour cream, 1 tablespoon at a time, beating well after each addition. (If the frosting should start to separate, mix it longer and don't add any more sour cream. If that doesn't fix it, add more confectioner's sugar 1 tablespoon at a time until it stabilizes.)

To assemble, remove the cooled cake from the springform pan by loosening the edges of the cake from the pan with a knife, unbuckling and removing the ring, lifting the cake from the pan bottom with a spatula, and peeling off the parchment paper. Set on a serving plate and spread frosting on top. Garnish with marigolds or husk cherries, if desired. The cake can be stored covered in the refrigerator 3–4 days.

Blueberry Sauce

This recipe is for when you're in the mood for blueberry pie, but you don't have enough time, blueberries, or inclination to justify the effort. I love it with tiny lowbush blueberries, but plump highbush blueberries work well too. Lightly sweetened, this sauce could not be simpler or more delicious. It's incredible over Connecticut Valley Vanilla Ice Cream or Maine Butter-milk and Sea Salt Ice Cream. If you're feeling slightly more ambitious, you can top it off with one or more Pie Crisps (page 78) for a charmingly deconstructed blueberry pie à la mode experience.

MAKES ABOUT 1½ CUPS

1 pound blueberries

¼ cup granulated sugar

1 teaspoon freshly squeezed lemon juice

Dash of cinnamon

In a small saucepan, bring the blueberries, sugar, lemon juice, and cinnamon to a simmer over medium heat. Reduce the heat to low and continue to simmer 8–12 minutes, stirring occasionally. Berries will release their juices with some remaining whole as the mixture thickens slightly. Remove from the heat and let cool. Store in a pint jar in the fridge for up to 1 month. Serve over ice cream with pie crisps.

Peach Ginger Compote

Here's a quick stovetop fruit topping that will elevate your ice cream game. Fresh ginger brightens ripe summer peaches and gives them a welcome zing. The ginger isn't meant to overpower here, just to embellish, but you can certainly increase the potency to your own taste. Serve over Connecticut Valley Vanilla Ice Cream (page 193) or Maine Buttermilk and Sea Salt Ice Cream (page 204) with Pie Crisps (page 78) on top.

MAKES ABOUT 1 CUP

1 pound peaches (3–4 medium)

½ cup granulated sugar

¼ teaspoon fresh ginger, peeled and grated with a microplane grater

2 teaspoons lemon juice, freshly squeezed

To peel the peaches, you can often remove the skin of really ripe peaches by using a paring knife to nick the skin and peel. Otherwise, the quickest way is to score an X on the bottom of the peaches, dunk them in boiling water for 30 seconds, and then dunk them in ice water to cool them down. The skins will slip right off.

Remove the peach pits and cut the peaches into slices or slim chunks. Combine the peaches, sugar, ginger, and lemon juice in a small saucepan. (If you don't have a microplane grater for the ginger, you can add a thick slice of ginger to the pot instead and fish it out after cooking.) Bring to a boil, then simmer over low heat 10–12 minutes until slightly thickened and syrupy. Let cool. Store in a jar in the refrigerator up to 1 week.

Honey Cornmeal Cake

Baked and boiled breads made with cornmeal were staples of the Native Algonquin tribes that inhabited the area now known as New England. These were the origins of our regional corn bread. By adding more sweetener, it's not much of a leap into cake territory. Here, I lean on local honey for sweetness and flavor. I love the complexity of wildflower honey, but you can also seek out single-source specialty honeys, like blueberry, cranberry, raspberry, apple blossom, and buckwheat. This rustic one-bowl cake tastes great with fresh fruit and a dollop of Greek yogurt on the side, or topped with any of the fruit sauces and compotes in this book, like Strawberry Rhubarb (page 39). You can also stir a few handfuls of fresh cranberries or blueberries into the batter, as the Native Americans might do.

SERVES 8–12

1 cup yellow cornmeal

1 cup all-purpose flour

¾ cup granulated sugar

1 teaspoon baking powder

¼ teaspoon baking soda

½ teaspoon salt

1 stick (½ cup) unsalted butter, melted

¼ cup honey

½ cup plain yogurt, preferably full fat

2 large eggs

Preheat the oven to 350°F. Grease a 9-inch round cake pan or 8 × 8-inch square pan.

Combine the dry ingredients in a large bowl with a whisk. Add the melted butter, honey, yogurt, and eggs. Stir with a wooden spoon until combined. Pour into the prepared pan and spread the batter evenly, smoothing the top.

Bake 25–30 minutes until golden and a toothpick inserted into the center comes out with only moist crumbs, no raw batter. Let cool. Store covered at room temperature for 2–3 days so it doesn't dry out.

Fall

*A*utumn is the undisputed crown jewel of New England with its glorious weather, bountiful harvests, and dazzling fall foliage. Cool nights and drier air offer a much needed respite from summer's heat and humidity. As the birds head south to warmer climes, New Englanders head north to the woods for blissfully bug-free hiking, mushroom foraging, and leaf-peeping. Sugar maples start off the show (late September in my neck of the woods) with brilliant orange flame-colored leaves. Red maples wax dramatic scarlet, while aspen, birch, and ash glow yellow. White oaks follow in burnished bronze. The days get shorter, the air a little crisper, like a fresh-picked apple. The light takes on a golden hue, the scent of wood smoke on the air. It's cozy sweater season, warm mittens cupping mugs of mulled cider, steam curling in the frosty air.

For food lovers, autumn offers the best of all worlds: the culmination of the summer harvest overlapping with fall favorites, like apples, pumpkins, and cranberries. Families flock to the local orchards for pick-your-own apples, hayrides, and warm cider doughnuts dusted with cinnamon sugar. We wander the pumpkin fields, sizing up the orange gourds until we find just the right one that speaks to our creative ambitions. And Massachusetts cranberry bogs are flooded so the floating berries can be more easily corralled.

This chapter is flush with fall baking inspiration, like Apple Cider Doughnut Cake (page 107) and the decadent Caramel Apple Tarts featured on the cover (page 93). Pumpkins claim their time in the sun with spooky Jack-o'-Lantern Hand Pies (page 125) and fragrantly spiced Pumpkin Whoopie Pies (page 115). Garnet cranberries gussy up all manner of baked goods with their vibrant tartness and festive color, like Cranberry Crumb Bars (page 103). Together with pears, they create a memorable Pear Cranberry Slab Pie (page 139).

But there's more. Autumn in New England also promises Concord grapes, local pears and quince, and nuts like shagbark hickory, black walnut, and butternut. Even root vegetables like carrots and parsnips (even turnips!) turn out some fantastic desserts. Sometimes it feels like there aren't enough days in the season to celebrate all that fall has to offer. Not to worry, most of these recipes can be made all throughout the wintertime, too. Fire up the wood stove and get cozy.

Apples

Though apples aren't native to North America, we've been growing and cooking with them for 400 years. The British introduced apples to New England by transporting the cuttings by ship to their colonial outposts. Over time, the trees spread. New England boasts several heirloom apple varieties that arose as chance seedlings from those original plantings or subsequent generations, like the Roxbury Russet and Rhode Island Greening (see sidebar).

Heirloom Apple Varieties of New England

Roxbury Russet: Grew from seed in the early 1600s in Roxbury, MA

Rhode Island Greening: Found in the mid-1600s in Newport, RI

Baldwin: Discovered in the mid-1700s in Wilmington, MA

Black Oxford: Appeared in the late 1700s in Paris, ME

Westfield Seek-No-Further: Originated around 1796 in Westfield, MA

Hubbardston Nonesuch: First recorded in 1832 in Hubbardston, MA

Northern Spy: Grown in the mid-1800s in NY from seeds brought from Salisbury, CT

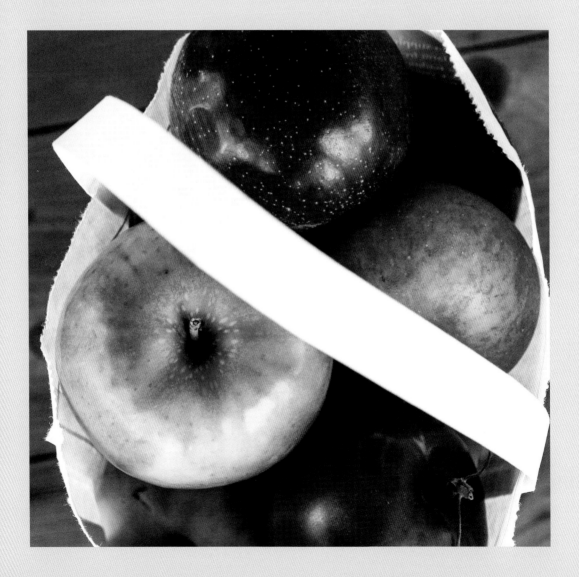

I always thought of McIntosh as the quintessential New England apple—tart and tender when fresh, saucy when cooked—so I was surprised to discover its origins are Canadian. It was a chance seedling found in Ontario in the late 1800s by farmer John McIntosh, but it's widely grown throughout Canada and New England alike. Both Cortlands and Macouns, descendants of the McIntosh, were bred at the New York State Agricultural Experiment Station in Geneva, along with many other popular apple varieties grown in New England today, like Jonagold and Empire.

Some apples are better for baking than others. Tart, crisp apples, like Northern Spy, Rhode Island Greening, and Granny Smith, are best for pies and crumbles. In the event you have a bag of mixed apples and no idea which are which, a combination of apples will give you a nice, round flavor (avoid McIntoshes, as they tend to cook down to mush—but they make a great applesauce). When in doubt, Cortlands are just about as good an all-purpose apple as you'll find, great in pies, sauces, dipped in caramel sauce, or straight off the tree. Apples can be stored at room temperature for short periods of time, but for longer term storage (more than a week), keep them in the refrigerator, preferably the crisper drawer in a bag with holes poked in it, to preserve their texture and moisture content.

Pumpkins and Squash

Winter squash and pumpkins are dietary staples of the Native Peoples of North America. Both English words were derived from Algonquin dialects: *pôhpukun* (Wampanoag) and *askútasquash* (Narragansett). The pumpkin is the state fruit of New Hampshire (yes, pumpkins and squash are fruits like melons). While big carving pumpkins are good for jack-o'-lanterns, stick to the smaller, sweeter specimens, like sugar pumpkins, for cakes and pie. Even butternut squash and other sweet winter squashes, like kabocha, red kuri, and buttercup, make excellent stand-ins. Roasting them in halves (cut-side-down at 350°F for about an hour) makes it easier to discard the seeds and scoop out the flesh. A quick whir in the food processor transforms slightly stringy flesh into a silky smooth puree, and an overnight strain removes excess moisture. But if this sounds like too much work, there's no shame in using canned pumpkin or squash.

Cranberries

Cranberries are another plant native to North America, found in the boggy areas of New England created by the receding glaciers of the last ice age. The berries were especially common in southeastern Massachusetts, where they were harvested by the Wampanoag and

Narragansett for food, medicine, and a natural dye well before the Pilgrims touched down in Plymouth. The cranberry was so named because, like its European cousin, the flowers resemble the head and neck of a crane. In Massachusetts, the cranberry harvest usually starts in late September and runs through October into early November. The bogs are flooded and air pockets inside the berries cause them to float to the surface where they can be collected. Look for fresh berries that are firm, shiny, and bright to dark red. Discard any that are soft or shriveled. They should literally bounce. Buy extra bags to freeze so you have a supply throughout the winter. Dried cranberries (or craisins) are another way to extend the season and their special sweet-tart flavor.

Concord Grapes

These beautifully aromatic dark purple-blue grapes with a translucent bloom were developed by Ephraim Wales Bull in 1849 on his farm in Concord, Massachusetts. By crossing native wild grapes with European varieties, he discovered a chance seedling that ripened early enough to escape the killing New England frosts. After its debut at the 1853 Boston Horticultural Society Exhibition, it won numerous awards and went on to become the juice and jelly darling of America. Concord grapes don't keep too long, so store them in the refrigerator and plan to use them within a couple of days. For a stunning and not-too-sweet take on this historic fruit, try the Concord Grape Sorbet (page 99).

Pears

Like apples, pears were also brought to New England by the British settlers. Although they haven't reached quite the same level of popularity as apples, I love them for their sweet taste and buttery texture when cooked. Early season Barletts and late season Boscs are my favorite varieties for baking, with tiny Seckels great for eating fresh. My advice: Buy whatever pears are on offer at your local farmers' market and ask if they're better for cooking, snacking, or both. You can hardly go wrong that way. When choosing pears, keep in mind that pears are picked unripe and they need time to slowly ripen off the tree, sometimes a week or so. Winter pears are ready when the neck (the slimmer part near the stem) gives a little when gently pressed. Early pears like Barletts turn from green to yellow when ripe. You can use pears in almost any recipe that calls for apples (just keep in mind that they cook more quickly).

Quince

Another relative of apples and pears, quince was once a common addition to the English cottage garden, but is now something of a culinary oddity. Greenish-yellow and knobby, the fruit emits a fragrant, fruity scent reminiscent of green apple Jolly Ranchers. Raw, the fruit is astringent and inedible. But poach slices slowly in sugar syrup, and you'll be rewarded with something really special, like a cross between a pear and some exotic fruit. Depending on the variety, the fruit sometimes turns pink to deep red with slow-cooking. To highlight this beautiful yet uncommon fruit, try the Quince Cardamom Upside-Down Cake (page 117). Store fruits in a bag with holes poked in it in the refrigerator for up to a week, maybe two.

Figs

While I wouldn't call fresh figs a typical New England ingredient (the trees usually succumb to the cold winters), dried figs are certainly common enough. Dried Black Mission figs are the main ingredient for Fig Newtons, a popular New England product. I've had luck keeping a fig tree alive by burying it underground for the winter. I dig a long, shallow grave, wrap the tree up in weed-suppressing fabric (or burlap), and wrestle it down into the ground, covering it back up with dirt and laying a board on top. I learned this trick from an elderly Italian fellow at Russo's market in Watertown, Massachusetts, before it closed. It worked very well when the tree was a small; it's much more challenging now that the tree is taller than I am. You can find fresh figs from time to time at farmers' markets, but they're highly perishable, so store them in the refrigerator and use as soon as possible. Dried figs are available in supermarkets year-round.

Root Vegetables

Grated root vegetables like carrots and parsnips make excellent additions to cakes, like the Celebration Carrot Cake (page 122). Even turnips can be mashed and added to spiced batters with excellent results. For the Eastham Turnip Snacking Cake (page 137), I was inspired by the sweet Cape Cod turnip (some say rutabaga) that is celebrated every year with a local festival in Eastham, Massachusetts. But the Macomber turnip (from Westport, Massachusetts) or even a standard-issue purple-top turnip will do. Root vegetables store very well (sometimes for months) in the crisper drawer of your refrigerator, so don't rule them out for winter indulgences too.

Caramel Apple Tarts

Just when you thought apple pie couldn't get any better, someone drizzled caramel over the top. The bitter, sweet, and salty flavors of the caramel work wonderfully alongside tart apples (and sometimes I'll throw in a handful of cranberries). These rustic individual tarts are so pretty, they could easily be served at any of the various holiday gatherings throughout the fall and winter. Make the caramel ahead of time and use the rest of the jar for sundaes and dipping raw apple slices.

SERVES 4-8

For the crust:

2 cups all-purpose flour

1 tablespoon granulated sugar

1 teaspoon table salt

1½ sticks (¾ cup) cold, unsalted butter, cut into 12 pieces

4-6 tablespoons ice water

For the filling:

2 pounds baking apples, like Northern Spy, Rhode Island Greening, or Granny Smith

1 teaspoon lemon juice, freshly squeezed

½ cup granulated sugar

1 tablespoon all-purpose flour

½ teaspoon ground cinnamon

Pinch of ground nutmeg

¼ cup fresh cranberries (optional)

1 large egg

For serving:

1 recipe Salted Caramel Sauce (page 224)

Make the caramel and let it chill in the refrigerator until ready to serve.

For the crust, combine the flour, sugar, and salt in the bowl of a food processor. Add the cold butter and process 10–15 seconds, until the butter pieces stop jumping around like popcorn. Stream 4 tablespoons (¼ cup) of the ice water through the feed tube with the machine running for 2–3 seconds. Add 1–2 more tablespoons of ice water as needed until the mixture just holds together when gently squeezed. (If you don't have a food processor, you can also work the butter into the dry ingredients with a stand mixer fitted with a paddle attachment, a pastry blender, or your fingers.)

Gather the dough together, folding it over once or twice to create layers. Form it into four reasonably equal disks, and wrap them in waxed paper, plastic wrap, or reusable wraps. Let rest in the refrigerator 20–30 minutes.

Preheat the oven to 425°F. Line a rimmed baking sheet with parchment paper.

For the filling, peel, core, and thinly slice the apples (I like to keep the slices in clusters that can be fanned out later). Place in a large bowl and drizzle with lemon juice.

In a small bowl, combine the sugar, flour, cinnamon, and nutmeg. Set aside.

Flour your counter and rolling pin well. Roll out the first disk of dough about 7 inches in diameter (slightly less than ¼ inch thick). Transfer the dough to the prepared pan by loosening it

from the counter with a bench scraper or spatula. Sprinkle ½ tablespoon of the sugar mixture in the middle of the dough. Arrange ¼ of the apples in the center of the dough, leaving a 1-inch margin around the edge. Sprinkle 1 tablespoon of the sugar mixture over the apples. Add ¼ of the cranberries. Fold the edges of the dough over the fruit in five or six equal sections, letting the dough overlap in the corners. Repeat with the three remaining dough disks. Divide the remaining sugar mixture among the tarts.

In a small bowl, whisk the egg with a teaspoon of water. Brush the egg wash over the crust.

Bake the tarts 15 minutes at 425°F, then reduce the heat to 375°F. Bake 30–35 minutes more until the juices bubble and the crust is golden brown. Remove from the oven and let cool slightly.

The tarts can be served warm or at room temperature. Serve them whole, halved, or cut into thirds for a more tailored distribution. Reheat the caramel gently in the microwave, if needed, and drizzle it over the tarts, with or without a scoop of vanilla or buttermilk ice cream. Pass the caramel at the table if anyone wants an extra drizzle or two. These tarts are best served the day they're made, but leftovers can be stored covered at room temperature 1–2 days or in the refrigerator 3–4 days.

Fresh Fig and Raspberry Newtons

Named for the city of Newton, Massachusetts, these soft cookies with the fruit centers were first manufactured in 1891 by Cambridgeport's F. A. Kennedy Steam Bakery (which later became part of Nabisco). The original recipe, an adaptation of the British fig roll, was made with dried figs, which are available year-round. My homemade homage showcases seasonally available fresh figs and fall raspberries, for a balance of sweet and tart. If you can't get your hands on fresh figs, you can substitute a sweet apple (like Gala or Fuji), peeled and grated up to the core, along with 1 tablespoon of granulated sugar and as much water as needed to keep the pan from getting dry. For best results, make these cookies at least a day ahead of time and store them in an airtight container so they soften and mellow like your favorite brand.

MAKES ABOUT 2 DOZEN

For the dough:

1¼ cups all-purpose flour

¾ cup whole wheat flour

1 teaspoon baking powder

½ teaspoon salt

1 stick (½ cup) unsalted butter, at room temperature

½ cup light brown sugar, firmly packed

½ teaspoon orange zest (shiny orange part only)

1 large egg, at room temperature

1 egg yolk, at room temperature

1 teaspoon vanilla extract

1 tablespoon milk

For the dough, whisk together the flours, baking powder, and salt in a medium bowl. Set aside.

Cream the butter and brown sugar for 2–3 minutes on medium-high speed until fluffy, scraping down the bottom and sides of the bowl as needed. Add the orange zest and mix until distributed. Add the egg plus the yolk and mix until incorporated, 1–2 minutes, until fluffy and lightened in color. Mix in the vanilla. Add the dry ingredients and mix on low speed until the dough starts to coalesce. With the machine running on low, slowly dribble in the milk and mix just until the dough comes together. The dough will be very soft.

Empty the dough onto a sheet of parchment paper. On a second sheet of parchment paper, draw a 12 × 12-inch square, and set that on top of the dough. Press down with your hands to flatten the dough. With a rolling pin, roll out the dough just beyond the marked dimensions, making sure to get all the way into the corners. Set the dough on a cookie sheet in the refrigerator to chill for 1 hour.

While the dough is chilling, combine the figs, raspberries, water, honey, and lemon juice in a small saucepan. Cook uncovered over medium-low heat, stirring frequently, 10–15 minutes until jammy and all the excess liquid has evaporated. Let cool. Pulse the mixture in a food processor 5–10 seconds to break up any larger pieces of fig. Transfer to a small bowl.

For the filling:

8 ounces fresh figs, stemmed, chopped (about 2 cups)

8 ounces raspberries (about 1⅓ cups)

¼ cup water

2 tablespoons honey

2 teaspoons freshly squeezed lemon juice

Preheat the oven to 325°F. Grease or line a cookie sheet with parchment paper.

Remove the dough from the refrigerator and set on the counter. Peel off the top sheet of parchment. Using a paring knife and ruler, trim the dough to a neat 12 × 12-inch square. Divide the dough into 4 equal columns, each 3 inches wide, and cut with a paring knife (use kitchen shears or scissors to cut through the parchment). You should have 4 (3-inch) strips with parchment backing.

Transfer one strip to the prepared pan, parchment side up (refrigerate the rest in the meantime). Gently peel off the parchment. Spoon or pipe the filling about ½ inch wide down the center of the strip the long way. With your hands, lift the long sides of the strip over the filling and towards each other, as if rolling it into a log. Press the dough together at the seam and on the ends to seal. Roll it over seam-side-down. No need to flatten the log, as it will do so as it bakes. Repeat with the remaining strips of dough, spacing at least 2 inches apart on the prepared pan.

Bake the logs 18–22 minutes until the dough is firm and dry when gently pressed, before it starts to crack. Remove from the oven and immediately cut into 1½-inch squares. Let cool completely.

For best results, let the cooled cookies sit in an airtight container overnight to soften before serving. They tend to get better the longer they sit. Store at room temperature or in the refrigerator if you prefer them cold for up to 1 week.

Variations

Apple Newtons: While the dough chills, peel and grate 4 medium apples and add to a small saucepan. Add 2 tablespoons granulated sugar, 2 tablespoons apple cider (or water), 1 teaspoon freshly squeezed lemon juice, and ¼ teaspoon ground cinnamon. Cook 10-15 minutes over medium-low heat until the apples are soft and all the excess water has evaporated. Proceed with assembly.

Fig Newtons: While the dough chills, stem 8 ounces of dried Black Mission figs and add them to a small saucepan with ¾ cup of water, ¼ cup applesauce, 1 tablespoon freshly squeezed orange juice, and 1 tablespoon honey. Bring to a simmer over medium-low heat, then reduce the heat to low and cook, covered, 10-15 minutes. Remove from the heat and let cool slightly. Pulse the mixture in a food processor 5-10 seconds to form a paste. Transfer to a small bowl and proceed with assembly.

Concord Grape Sorbet

The Concord grape, of Welch's grape juice and peanut butter and jelly fame, was developed in Concord, Massachusetts, in 1849 and soon took the world by storm. This sorbet recipe, inspired by a favorite jam I like to make, lets the pure flavor of the historic Concord grape sing. I've intentionally kept this sorbet on the less sweet side to really bring out the complex flavor of the grapes. Try it alone or alongside vanilla ice cream or Salted Oat and Walnut Sandies (page 14). A food mill, basically a hand-cranked colander, is useful for this recipe to strain out the seeds and skins. For best results, start the day before you want to serve it to allow enough time to make the base, churn, and freeze it.

MAKES ABOUT 1 QUART

2 pounds Concord grapes, stemmed (about 2 dry quarts)

⅔ cup granulated sugar

1 tablespoon lemon juice, freshly squeezed

Pinch of salt

Mash the grapes in a medium saucepan with a potato masher. Stir in the sugar, lemon juice, and salt. Cook over medium heat, stirring occasionally, until it comes to a boil. Reduce the heat to medium-low and simmer 5 minutes. Remove from the heat and let cool.

Run the mixture through a food mill set over a large bowl in the sink (I use the disk with the medium-sized holes). Alternatively, you can pulse the mixture in a food processor to break up the fruit and then strain it through a standard mesh strainer set over a large bowl in the sink.

Chill the mixture in the refrigerator until cold (4–6 hours).

Pour the mixture into an ice cream maker and process according to the manufacturer's instructions. Transfer to a container and freeze at least 6–8 hours. If you don't have an ice cream machine, try the food processor method or the low-tech version (page 191).

Pumpkin Pie with Apple Cider Crust

My husband loves pumpkin pie so much, he's known to bake them two at a time: one for himself and one for everybody else. In fact, what you see in the photo is what happened when he discovered unexpected pumpkin pie one morning. He had worked late the night before, and I'd forgotten to write a note threatening bodily harm if he touched that pie before my photo shoot. I came downstairs with my camera the next morning just in time to catch him going back for a second piece of pumpkin pie for breakfast! Be sure to refrigerate your pie until it's cold, cold, cold before serving. This version contains apple cider and a bit of cinnamon in the crust for a little extra fall flavor.

SERVES 8–12

For the crust:

1¼ cups all-purpose flour

1 teaspoon granulated sugar

½ teaspoon salt

⅛ teaspoon ground cinnamon

6 tablespoons cold, unsalted butter, cut into 6 pieces

3–4 tablespoons cold apple cider

For the filling:

1 (15-ounce) can or 2 cups cooked, pureed pumpkin (see note)

3 large eggs

½ cup light brown sugar, firmly packed

⅓ cup granulated sugar

1 tablespoon flour

¾ teaspoon ground ginger

½ teaspoon ground cinnamon

½ teaspoon ground nutmeg

¼ teaspoon ground allspice

If using fresh pumpkin, be sure to drain the puree in a fine-meshed sieve set over a bowl while you prepare the other ingredients. (Canned pumpkin does not need to be drained.)

For the crust, mix the flour, sugar, salt, and cinnamon in a food processor. Add the butter pieces and process until the butter stops jumping around like popcorn, 10–15 seconds. Add 2 tablespoons of the apple cider and process briefly. Dribble in the remaining 1–2 tablespoons of apple cider as needed with the machine running until the mixture starts to come together. (If you don't have a food processor, you can also work the butter into the dry ingredients with a stand mixer fitted with a paddle attachment, a pastry blender, or your fingers.)

Turn the mixture out onto a sheet of waxed paper, plastic wrap, or reusable wrap. Gently form it into a disk. Fold it in half, then in half again, and then reflatten into a disk. Wrap and refrigerate for 30 minutes.

Preheat the oven to 450°F. Set aside a 9-inch pie plate.

For the filling, whisk the eggs slightly in a large bowl. Beat in the sugars. Add the flour, spices, and salt, and stir with a wooden spoon to combine. Stir in the pumpkin, then the warm milk.

Roll out the dough on a floured surface to about a 12-inch diameter. Transfer to the pie plate and crimp the edges. Pour in the filling and set on the middle rack of the oven. Bake for

⅛ teaspoon ground cloves

½ teaspoon salt

½ cup warm milk, preferably 1% (but not skim)

10 minutes at 450°F, then reduce the heat to 350°F and bake 55–60 minutes more, until the crust is golden-brown and the filling is gently puffed all the way to the middle. (If the crust starts taking on too much color, you can cover the edges with foil.)

Remove from the oven and let cool at room temperature. Refrigerate at least 6 hours before serving, and preferably overnight. Slice and serve with lightly sweetened whipped cream.

How to Prepare Fresh Pumpkin and Squash for Pie

Small pumpkins, like Sugar, New England Pie, and Long Pie pumpkins, are sweeter and have more flavor than big, bland carving pumpkins. But you can also enlist a wide variety of winter squashes. Butternut, Kabocha, and Red Kuri are excellent stand-ins. Just halve the gourds, roast them cut side down on a lightly oiled, rimmed baking sheet, in a 375°F oven. Roast for 45 minutes to 1 hour until soft. Let them cool slightly, then scoop out the seeds and discard. Scrape the flesh out of the skins and puree in a food processor until smooth. Drain in a colander set over a bowl for at least an hour, and preferably overnight, to remove the excess liquid.

The History of Pumpkin Pie

Pumpkin pie is a distinctly American invention that started right here in New England. British pumpkin pies existed, but they were made by layering strips of fried pumpkin rather than mashing cooked pumpkin with milk, sugar, spices, and egg. A recipe for "Pumpkin Pudding" baked in a crust can be found in the first truly American cookbook, *American Cookery*, published in Hartford, Connecticut, in 1796 by Amelia Simmons. It bears a striking resemblance to modern Thanksgiving pumpkin pies.

Cranberry Crumb Bars

For a beautiful combination of sweet and tart, look no further than these buttery streusel bars to celebrate the New England cranberry harvest. I also add a little bit of apple to tame the tartness. I prefer McIntoshes because they cook down saucy and meld with the cranberries, but you could use any other type of apple or even a ripe pear. You'll barely even notice it's there. Then prepare to eat all the bars within a few days, as the moisture from the fruit tends to uncrisp the topping over time.

MAKES 16 SQUARES

For the crust and topping:

2 cups all-purpose flour, divided

¾ cup light brown sugar, firmly packed

½ teaspoon baking powder

¼ teaspoon salt

10 tablespoons cold unsalted butter

1 large egg

¼ teaspoon vanilla extract

For the filling:

1 apple, peeled

2 cups cranberries, fresh or frozen (if frozen, thawed then drained)

⅔ cup granulated sugar

1 tablespoon cornstarch

1 teaspoon vanilla extract

¼ teaspoon ground cardamom

Preheat the oven to 350°F. Grease an 8 × 8-inch pan or line with parchment paper.

Measure 1½ cups of flour and pour it into the bowl of a food processor. Add the brown sugar, baking powder, and salt. Pulse the motor to combine. Add the cold butter, and process 15–20 seconds, until the butter is incorporated and the mixture holds together when gently squeezed. (If you don't have a food processor, you can also work the butter into the dry ingredients with a stand mixer fitted with a paddle attachment, a pastry blender, or your fingers.)

Pour ⅓ of the mixture into a small bowl (1 heaping cup) and set aside for the topping. Leave the rest in the food processor bowl. Add the remaining ½ cup of flour and the egg. Blend just until it starts to come together into a dough, 5–10 seconds. Firmly press the dough into the bottom of the prepared pan. Reserve the vanilla for the topping.

For the filling, grate all four sides of the peeled apple on the large holes of a box grater until you hit the core. You should have about 1 cup of grated apple. Toss the apple with the cranberries, sugar, cornstarch, vanilla, and cardamom in a medium bowl until well coated. Arrange evenly on top of the dough in the pan.

For the topping, dribble the vanilla over the reserved flour mixture. Stir until crumbly. Sprinkle over the cranberry filling.

Bake 40–50 minutes until the filling is bubbly and the top is golden. Remove from the oven and let cool completely. Cut into squares and serve as soon as possible, as the crumble will absorb the moisture from the filling over time. If you must, store them loosely covered in the refrigerator so there's airflow.

Plum Raspberry Pandowdy

A pandowdy is an old-fashioned baked fruit dessert, often made with apples and a top crust only. I had always thought the name was related to the dish's unfashionable, homespun appearance, as if it were all thrown together at the last minute using whatever pan happened to be available. But, in fact, "dowdying" refers to breaking up the crust halfway through the baking time and partially submerging it in the fruit to continue cooking. It gives the dessert a more interesting rustic look and has an additional thickening effect on the filling. Here, I've elevated Italian prune plums into the spotlight (though other larger plums can be substituted), along with a few handfuls of fall raspberries and a bit of apple. Because plums are so juicy, the fluffy buttermilk biscuit dough does double duty as shortcake, soaking up any delectable juices left behind in the bowl.

SERVES 6–8

For the filling:

1½ pounds Italian prune plums (ripe but firm), stemmed, pitted, unpeeled (about 11–12 small plums)

1 cup raspberries

½ baking apple, like Northern Spy, Granny Smith, or Gravenstein, peeled, grated

½ cup granulated sugar, plus 1 tablespoon for topping

¼ cup cornstarch

1 tablespoon lemon juice, freshly squeezed

½ teaspoon vanilla extract

½ teaspoon ground nutmeg

¼ teaspoon ground ginger

⅛ teaspoon ground cinnamon

Preheat the oven to 375°F. Butter the inside of a deep-dish 9-inch pie plate or 8 × 8-inch baking dish.

For the filling, cut the plums into quarters, then slice each quarter into 2- to 3½-inch-thick wedges. Add to the prepared baking dish along with the raspberries. Grate half of the peeled apple on the large holes of a box grater and add to the filling. Gently fold in the sugar, cornstarch, lemon juice, vanilla, and spices. Set aside.

For the topping, add the flour, baking powder, salt, and baking soda to the bowl of a food processor. Pulse to combine. Add the butter and pulse until the mixture forms a coarse meal, 15–30 seconds. Add the buttermilk through the feed tube and pulse several times until a scrappy dough forms. (If you don't have a food processor, you can cut the butter into the dry ingredients in a mixing bowl with a pastry blender, fork and knife, or your fingers.)

Turn the dough onto the counter and gently fold the dough over on itself three or four times, until it comes together. If the dough seems too dry, drizzle a tiny bit more buttermilk over the dry areas and gently knead again once or twice. Roll the dough about ½ inch thick and 8–9 inches in diameter. Set the biscuit dough on top of the fruit, tucking any

For the crust:

2 cups all-purpose flour

1 teaspoon baking powder

½ teaspoon fine sea salt

¼ teaspoon baking soda

1½ sticks (¾ cup) unsalted
butter, cut into 12 pieces

½ cup buttermilk, plus 1
teaspoon for topping

Sugar, for topping

overhanging edges down into the fruit. Brush the top with buttermilk and sprinkle with sugar.

Bake uncovered until the fruit is bubbling and the topping is golden brown, 40–45 minutes. At the 30-minute mark, pull the pandowdy out of the oven and break up the crust with a spatula, partially submerging the pieces, then continue cooking for the remainder of the baking time. Let cool at least 10 minutes.

Serve the pandowdy warm or at room temperature with vanilla or buttermilk ice cream. Leftovers can be stored covered in the refrigerator 3–4 days.

Apple Cider Doughnut Cake

Nothing says autumn like piping hot cider doughnuts fresh from your local apple orchard, cinnamon sugar dusting your sweater. But eventually the orchards will close for the season, while your doughnut cravings linger deep into the winter months. If you're not in the mood to mess around with hot oil, this simple cake version of the fried classic does the trick and feeds a crowd. It's basically a giant doughnut made in a bundt pan. The thick slices are equally good as breakfast or a snacking cake to take with tea or apple cider. They're also fantastic topped with vanilla or buttermilk ice cream and salted caramel sauce (page 224).

SERVES 12–16

For the cake:

1 tablespoon vegetable or canola oil, for the pan

1 stick (½ cup) unsalted butter, melted

1 cup light brown sugar, firmly packed

1 teaspoon vanilla extract

3 large eggs, at room temperature

2½ cups all-purpose flour

2 teaspoons baking powder

½ teaspoon baking soda

¾ teaspoon ground nutmeg

½ teaspoon ground cinnamon

½ teaspoon salt

1 cup apple cider

½ cup crème fraîche (or sour cream)

Preheat the oven to 350°F. Brush a large bundt pan with oil, taking care to cover the entire interior area.

In a large bowl, mix the melted butter with the brown sugar and vanilla. Whisk in the eggs one at a time. Add the flour, baking powder, baking soda, nutmeg, cinnamon, and salt to the bowl. Start whisking in the middle of the bowl to incorporate the dry ingredients and, when it gets too thick to stir easily, add half of the apple cider. Continue whisking, again adding the rest of the apple cider when it gets hard to stir. Finally, whisk in the crème fraîche until well combined. Pour the batter into the bundt pan.

Bake 45–55 minutes, until a toothpick inserted into the deepest part of the cake comes out clean. Remove from the oven and let cool slightly in the pan while making the syrup.

Add the butter, brown sugar, and apple cider to a small saucepan set over medium heat. Stir occasionally until the butter melts and the mixture becomes bubbly. Lower the heat slightly and simmer 1–2 minutes until the mixture is slightly thickened and reduced to about 2 tablespoons. Transfer to small bowl or ramekin.

In another small bowl, stir together the sugar and cinnamon.

Brush the exposed bottom surface of the cake with the apple cider syrup. Sprinkle generously with cinnamon-sugar. Invert a serving plate over the top of the pan and, gripping the two together firmly with oven mitts, flip so that the cake

For the syrup:

1 tablespoon unsalted butter

1 tablespoon light brown sugar, firmly packed

2 tablespoons apple cider

For the topping:

2 tablespoons granulated sugar

½ teaspoon ground cinnamon

pan is now right-side-up on the plate. If the cake doesn't release from the pan right away, let it sit a few minutes to let gravity help. Once the cake is out of its pan, let it cool completely.

Brush the top and sides of the cake with the apple cider glaze and sprinkle generously with cinnamon sugar. Serve plain with hot mulled cider or dressed up with a scoop of Connecticut Valley Vanilla Ice Cream or Maine Buttermilk and Sea Salt Ice Cream and warm Salted Caramel (page 224) for a seasonal-themed ice cream sundae. Leftovers can be stored, covered, at room temperature for 3–4 days.

Maple Caramel Corn

Popcorn is a different type of corn than the sweet corn we savor off the cob in the summer-time or flint corn that's ground into cornmeal. It has a unique structure that, when dried and then heated, causes a pressurized buildup of steam that ends with the interior starch exploding outwards up to 40 times its original size. In North America, the Algonquins made popcorn balls with maple syrup. In a similar spirit, this recipe has you cook a maple syrup-based caramel to pour over popcorn, which, once cool, can be broken into bite-sized clusters, salty and sweet.

SERVES 4-6

1 tablespoon vegetable or canola oil

¼ cup plain popcorn kernels

½ teaspoon fine sea salt, divided

½ cup maple syrup (the darker, the better)

¼ cup granulated sugar

4 tablespoons unsalted butter

Heat the oil and 2 dried popcorn kernels in a medium heavy-bottomed saucepan covered with a lid over medium heat. When both kernels pop (after 2–3 minutes), add the rest of the popcorn kernels and cover with the lid. Cook for 2–5 minutes, shaking the pot frequently while clamping the lid onto the pot with oven mitts, until the popping slows to 2–3 seconds between pops. Remove from the heat. (You can also pop the corn with an air-popper, if you prefer.)

Pour the popcorn onto a large, rimmed baking sheet and discard any unpopped kernels. Sprinkle the popcorn with half the salt and let cool while making the caramel.

Stir the maple syrup, sugar, and butter in a small heavy-bottomed saucepan over medium-low heat until the butter melts. Stop stirring and clip a candy thermometer to the pot and make sure the sensor is touching the mixture but not the bottom of the pot. (You may need to tip one side of the pot up a bit so the liquid pools deeply enough to get an accurate reading.)

Continue cooking for 10–15 minutes until the temperature reaches 300°F. If the mixture threatens to boil over, reduce the heat to low. The temperature will rise very slowly at first, but then shoot up quickly around the 280°F mark. Stay alert.

The History of Popcorn

Popcorn was the first type of corn to be domesticated in Central America about 9,000 years ago. It was developed from teosinte, a wild Mexican grass. The Aztecs used popcorn for food and decoration. To make it, dried cobs were tossed directly into the fire where some popped kernels remained attached to the cob while others would fly out wildly. Extra points if you caught them in midair! (Don't try this at home unless you want to burn your house down for the holidays.) All other types of corn, like sweet, flint, and dent, are descended from popcorn.

Remove the pot from the heat at 300°F and remove the thermometer. Carefully pour the caramel over the popcorn (it will be searingly hot). Sprinkle the remaining salt over the caramel. Do not touch the caramel until it has cooled at least 10–15 minutes and hardened.

When fully cool, break up the caramel corn into clusters and store in an airtight container for 4–5 days.

Boozy Pear Walnut Bread Pudding with Hot Buttered Rum Sauce

Pears are too often neglected in fall desserts, overshadowed by the more popular apple. But pears can replace apples in many desserts (though you might want to cut back on the sugar and cooking time, depending on the recipe). I love their sweet flavor in this bread pudding paired with crunchy walnuts and a heady rum sauce. You can use fresh bread or stale bread, just double the soaking time for stale. If you're a black walnut lover, this would be a good place to use them. You could also sub in local hickory nuts or butternuts if you have a source.

SERVES 6–8

For the pudding:

½ pound loaf Italian, French, or farm-style white bread, tough crusts removed

2 large eggs

⅓ cup granulated sugar, plus 1 tablespoon for the topping

1 cup milk (not skim)

1 cup heavy cream

3 tablespoons melted butter

1 teaspoon vanilla extract

2 tablespoons dark rum

¼ teaspoon kosher salt

1½ teaspoons ground cinnamon

3 ripe pears, like Bartlett, Bosc, or Anjou (I peel Boscs, but leave Bartletts and Anjous unpeeled)

½ cup chopped walnuts

Nutmeg, for sprinkling (preferably freshly grated)

Preheat the oven to 350°F. Butter an 8 × 8-inch deep-dish baking dish (2-quart).

For the pudding, cube the bread into ¾-inch pieces and place them in the buttered baking dish.

Whisk the eggs in a large bowl. Whisk in the sugar. Stir in the milk, cream, butter, vanilla, rum, and salt. Pour the cream mixture evenly over the bread. Sprinkle the cinnamon on top and let soak 15–20 minutes.

Meanwhile, cut the pears into quarters lengthwise and cut out the core by shaving off the interior edge with the seeds. Cut the quarters into ½-inch cubes. Scatter ⅓ of the diced pears on top, then flip everything over with a spatula. Let soak 15–20 more minutes.

For the sauce:

2 large egg yolks

1 cup heavy cream

½ cup light brown sugar, firmly packed

2 tablespoons dark rum

⅛ teaspoon kosher salt

2 tablespoons unsalted butter

For the sauce, set a medium bowl next to the stove with a standard mesh sieve over the bowl. Whisk the yolks in a medium saucepan off heat. Slowly whisk the cream into the yolks. Whisk in the sugar, rum, and salt. Set the pan over medium-low heat and cook 8–12 minutes, stirring frequently, until it comes to a bare simmer and thickens enough to coat the back of the spoon thinly. Pour the mixture through the sieve into the bowl. Remove the sieve and stir in the butter. Let cool. Store in the refrigerator until ready to serve.

Scatter the remaining diced pears and chopped walnuts over the top of the pudding. Sprinkle with nutmeg.

Bake 55–60 minutes until the center of the custard is set and the top is golden brown. Let cool at least 20 minutes before serving. Serve with hot buttered rum sauce, gently warmed in the microwave or on the stove, or vanilla ice cream. Leftovers can be stored covered in the refrigerator for 4–5 days.

Pumpkin Whoopie Pies

I'd like to shake the hand of whoever came up with the idea to take two regional classics—whoopie pies and pumpkin bread—and smoosh them together with cream cheese frosting into one super-duper New England dessert. You cannot go wrong with these pumpkin whoopie pies. The spicing is subtle yet festive, letting the brightness of the pumpkin and tanginess of the cream cheese share the spotlight. You can use canned pumpkin or fresh roasted, pureed pumpkin or squash, like butternut. It's worth letting the fresh stuff drain in a fine-mesh strainer over a bowl for at least an hour to remove any extra liquid. This will ensure your cakes don't spread too much in the oven. If you don't eat dairy, you can still enjoy these by omitting the filling and serving the cakes with a dairy-free glaze, like 1 cup confectioner's sugar mixed with 2 tablespoons apple cider.

MAKES 16–18

For the cakes:

2 cups all-purpose flour

½ teaspoon baking powder

½ teaspoon baking soda

½ teaspoon salt

1 teaspoon ground cinnamon

½ teaspoon ground ginger

¼ teaspoon ground cloves

1⅓ cups light brown sugar, firmly packed

½ cup vegetable oil

2 large eggs

1 cup pureed pumpkin, fresh or canned

Preheat the oven to 350°F. Grease or line two cookie sheets with parchment paper.

For the cakes, whisk the flour, baking powder, baking soda, salt, and spices together in a medium bowl. In a large bowl, whisk together the brown sugar, oil, eggs, and pumpkin. Add the dry ingredients to the wet and stir until combined.

Drop the batter in heaping tablespoon-sized dollops spaced 1½–2 inches apart (a 1-ounce cookie scoop works great here). The batter should slump a bit when scooped rather than hold its original shape like a scoop of ice cream. If it's too thick, add 1–2 tablespoons of water.

Bake 11–13 minutes. For best results, bake one cookie sheet at a time on the center rack so the tops don't crack. Remove from the oven when the centers are set and spring back when gently pressed. Let them sit on the hot pan for 5 minutes before transferring to racks to cool. Repeat with the second and third batch. Let cool completely before filling.

For the filling:

1 stick (½ cup) unsalted butter, at cool room temperature

2¼ cups confectioner's sugar, sifted

1 (8-ounce) package cream cheese

Pinch of salt

For the filling, beat the butter with an electric mixer (preferably fitted with a paddle attachment) until no lumps remain. Add the sifted confectioner's sugar in two or three batches, and beat on low to start, then increase to medium-high until combined. Add the cold cream cheese and salt. Mix until smooth and fluffy.

To assemble, wait until the cakes are fully cooled. Match up similarly sized cakes. Spoon a heaping tablespoon of filling and place in the center of the flat side of one of the cakes (again, a 1-ounce cookie scoop is the perfect tool). Sandwich another on top, and gently press and twist until the filling reaches the edges. Repeat for the rest.

Serve cold. Store, loosely covered (so the cakes don't get too sticky), in the refrigerator for up to 3 days or freeze.

Quince Cardamom Upside-Down Cake

///

Quince, a fruit related to apples and pears, was first introduced to New England by the British in the 1600s. Its high pectin content was highly valued for jam, making it a staple in the colonial cottage garden. Quince is also used in Armenian, Persian, and other Middle Eastern cookery. These days, quince is often passed over due to its knobby appearance and hard, tannic flesh when raw. But steep thin slices slowly in a sweet syrup, and you can coax out their perfumy flavor and, depending on the variety, a rosy color that deepens with cooking. You can find quince at the occasional New England orchard (try Westward Orchards in Harvard, Massachusetts; Rocky Brook Orchard in Middletown, Rhode Island; or Champlain Orchards in Shoreham, Vermont). The harvest window is short—start checking around in September, though you'll probably have better luck in October. If you can't find quince, this cake is also really delicious with pears, which don't require the long precooking that quinces do (see variation).

SERVES 6–8

For the topping:

1 pound quince (like Smyrna or Pineapple, about 2 medium), peeled

1 teaspoon lemon juice, freshly squeezed

¼ cup granulated sugar

1 cup apple cider

2 tablespoons butter

Pinch of cinnamon

For the cake:

1¼ cups all-purpose flour

1 teaspoon baking powder

1 teaspoon ground cardamom

¼ teaspoon table salt

6 tablespoons unsalted butter, melted

Preheat the oven to 350°F. Set aside a medium 9- or 10-inch oven-safe nonstick skillet with a lid (not cast iron, since the metal can react to the acidity of some types of quince).

Core the quince by cutting into quarters and making a shallow V-cut to remove the woody core from the interior edge. Slice the quince thinly. Combine the sliced quince and lemon juice in a medium bowl.

In a measuring cup, stir the sugar into the apple cider until dissolved.

On the stovetop, melt the butter in the skillet. Add the quince slices and pour the cider mixture over the fruit. Sprinkle with cinnamon. Bring the mixture to a simmer over medium heat, then turn the heat down to medium-low. Cover with the lid and cook 15 minutes. Remove the lid and cook 30 minutes, until the quince is tender when pierced with a fork. Remove from the heat. (If you don't have an oven-safe skillet, you can transfer the quince to a cake pan, arranging the slices decoratively, if you wish.)

⅔ cup granulated sugar

1 large egg

½ cup milk

1 teaspoon vanilla extract

For the cake, whisk together the flour, baking powder, cardamom, and salt in a medium bowl.

In a large bowl, stir together the melted butter and sugar with a wooden spoon until combined. Add the egg and beat well. In a measuring cup, stir together the milk and vanilla. Add ½ of the dry ingredients to the butter mixture and stir until combined. Slowly add the milk mixture and stir until homogenous. Add the rest of the dry ingredients and mix again. Gently pour the batter over the quince.

Bake 25–30 minutes until the cake is set in the middle (check with a toothpick). Remove from the oven and let cool 20 minutes. Gently loosen the fruit from the bottom of the pan with a spatula, then unmold onto a serving plate by inverting the plate over the pan, clamping the two together tightly with oven mitts, and flipping.

Serve warm or room temperature. The cake can be stored covered at room temperature 2–3 days.

Variation

Pear Cardamom Upside-Down Cake: Peel and core 2 pears by quartering them along the core and using a paring knife to shave off the interior corner edge, including the seeds. Cut the quarters into thin wedges. Melt the butter in a medium oven-safe nonstick skillet. Substitute 2 tablespoons firmly packed light brown sugar for the granulated sugar, and stir it into the butter. Add the lemon juice, cinnamon, and only 2 tablespoons of apple cider (or water). Stir until well combined. Remove from the heat and arrange the pears in the pan on top of the sugar mixture (or transfer to a 9-inch cake pan if you prefer). Proceed with the cake instructions.

Joe Froggers

These delightfully addictive molasses spice cookies hail from the coastal town of Marblehead, Massachusetts. There Joseph Brown (a former slave) and his wife, Lucretia, owned a lively tavern in the early 1800s. Lucretia would cook up these gingerbread cookies for the rough-and-tumble sailors that were their regulars. Her original version was said to be made with lard, seawater, and cooked in a cast iron pan. This recipe uses butter, sea salt, and a less laborious cooking process (i.e., cookie sheets), but readers are welcome to experiment with the original parameters.

**MAKES ABOUT 1 DOZEN
(RECIPE CAN BE DOUBLED)**

4 tablespoons unsalted butter, at room temperature

½ cup light brown sugar, firmly packed

½ cup molasses

1¾ cups all-purpose flour

½ teaspoon baking soda

¾ teaspoon ground ginger

¼ teaspoon ground nutmeg

¼ teaspoon ground cloves

⅛ teaspoon ground allspice

¾ teaspoon fine sea salt

2 tablespoons hot water

2 tablespoons dark rum

Preheat the oven to 375°F. Grease or line two cookie sheets with parchment paper.

With an electric mixer (preferably fitted with a paddle attachment), cream the butter on medium speed until smooth, about 1 minute. Scraping down the bottom and sides of the bowl with a rubber spatula as needed, add the brown sugar and continue beating on medium, 1–2 minutes. Add the molasses and beat a few minutes more.

In a medium bowl, sift together the flour, baking soda, ginger, nutmeg, cloves, and allspice. In a small bowl, stir the salt into the hot water until dissolved. Add the rum to the salt water.

Add half of the dry ingredients to the butter mixture, and mix on low speed just until combined, scraping down the bottom and sides of the bowl as needed. With the machine running, add the rum mixture gradually, mixing until combined. Add the rest of the dry ingredients, and mix well. The dough will be very soft and sticky.

History of Joe Froggers

In the early 1800s, Joseph and Lucretia Brown ran Black Joe's Tavern for more than 30 years out of their saltbox home on what came to be known as Gingerbread Hill in Marblehead, Massachusetts. The tavern served a mixed clientele of hard-living sailors and laborers of all colors. Joseph, who was half Black and half Wampanoag, was a former slave who gained his freedom by serving out his master's son's enlistment in the Revolutionary War. Lucretia (known as Aunt 'Crese) was the daughter of former slaves. She cooked up giant gingerbread cookies spiked with rum for her customers, as big as the lily pads on the nearby pond (hence the name). Because the cookies never went stale and ginger was thought to combat seasickness, sailors often brought them out to sea. The cookies are most likely a popular adaption of "Joe floggers," the pancake-like provisions that were staples on North Atlantic fishing vessels and rumored to have Viking origins.

With a paper towel, oil a 1-ounce cookie scoop or a tablespoon and dip in a small bowl of flour to prevent sticking. Scoop the dough (one level scoop or a heaping tablespoon) onto the prepared pans spaced 3 inches apart, reflouring the utensils each time. Press the bottom of a large mason jar or glass bowl (also oiled and floured) on top of each cookie until it's about ¼ inch thick and 3½ inches in diameter.

Bake 11–13 minutes until the tops of the cookies start to crack, the edges are set, but the centers are still soft. Let the cookies cool on the pan, where they will continue to firm up. Cookies can be stored covered at room temperature for weeks.

Celebration Carrot Cake
with Cream Cheese Frosting

Some layer cakes are a lot of work for results that just taste okay. This is not one of those cakes. I make this carrot cake for my husband's birthday every year, and it never disappoints. Fluffy and moist (but not sodden), it just might be the perfect cake for any occasion. Nuts are totally optional. For best results, let the butter and cream cheese for the frosting sit out at room temperature to soften for several hours beforehand for a silky, lump-free texture. This frosting recipe makes a generous amount, enough for a messy crumb coat, a pristine finishing coat, and even a little extra to pipe if you wish, so don't be stingy. Slather any extra on graham crackers or sandwich between oatmeal cookies. You'll either thank me or hate me later, probably both.

SERVES 12–16

For the cake:

2½ cups granulated sugar

1½ cups vegetable or canola oil

4 large eggs, separated

⅓ cup hot water

2½ cups all-purpose flour, plus 1 tablespoon for dusting pans

1½ teaspoons baking powder

½ teaspoon baking soda

¼ teaspoon salt

1 teaspoon ground nutmeg

1 teaspoon ground cinnamon

½ teaspoon ground cloves

1½ cups grated carrots (3–4 medium carrots)

1 cup chopped walnuts (optional)

Preheat the oven to 350°F. Grease two 9-inch circular cake pans and line with circles of parchment paper.

For the cake, mix the sugar and oil in a large bowl with a sturdy wooden spoon until well blended. Beat in the 4 egg yolks. Add the hot water and mix well.

In another large bowl, sift together the flour, baking powder, baking soda, salt, and spices. Beat the dry ingredients into the sugar mixture just until combined. Stir in the carrots and walnuts, if using. The batter will be very thick.

In a medium bowl, beat the egg whites with an electric mixer fitted with the whisk attachment on medium-high until they look smooth and dense, and form stiff peaks that don't droop when the beaters are lifted, 3–4 minutes. Stir about a quarter of the egg whites directly into the batter to loosen it up. Then fold in the rest of the egg whites with a rubber spatula, lifting up the batter from the bottom of the bowl and gently depositing it on top, rotating the bowl as you go, until no streaks remain.

Divide the batter equally into the two prepared cake pans and lightly smooth the tops. Bake 45–50 minutes, or until a toothpick inserted into the center comes out clean. Let cool completely. (Cakes may be wrapped tightly in plastic wrap, slipped back into their pans, and stored in the refrigerator for 2–3 days.)

For the frosting:

2 sticks (1 cup) unsalted butter, at cool room temperature

2 (8-ounce) packages cream cheese, at cool room temperature (not light or whipped)

1¼ pounds (5 cups) confectioner's sugar, sifted

Pinch of fine sea salt

2 cups (8 ounces) chopped walnuts, to decorate the sides (optional)

For the frosting, beat the softened butter and cream cheese in a large bowl with an electric mixer (preferably fitted with a paddle attachment). Continue beating 3–4 minutes, scraping the sides and bottom of the bowl often, until very smooth. Sift the confectioner's sugar into a large bowl (sifting is very important to prevent lumps). Add half of the confectioner's sugar and mix until smooth, starting at low speed and then gradually increasing to medium. Mix in the rest of the confectioner's sugar and the salt until smooth.

To assemble, remove the cakes from the pans by loosening the edges with a knife and inverting the pans over a rack. Peel off the parchment paper, and arrange one of the cake layers on a plate or pedestal. (I dab a tablespoon of frosting underneath to hold it in place.) Spread thickly with frosting and stack the second layer on top. Frost the sides, filling in the gaps between the two cakes, then frost the top. If you find you're getting crumbs in the frosting, apply about half of the total frosting in a thin coat on the whole cake, and then refrigerate for an hour. That will lock in the crumbs so that you can use the remaining frosting to give it a final, crumb-free coat.

Decorate the sides of the cake with chopped walnuts by carefully tilting the cake slightly and pressing a handful of nuts into the frosting, letting any loose pieces fall onto a plate set underneath. Repeat until the sides are well covered. Refrigerate and serve cold. Store leftovers, covered, in the refrigerator for 3–4 days.

Jack-o'-Lantern Hand Pies

Halloween is the most festive time of the year for these mini-pumpkin tartlets, but you can make them anytime you have a surplus of pumpkin or winter squash. Etching the jack-o'-lantern faces is fun, fiddly work, but if you're not super-crafty, you can skip it and cut decorative steam vents instead. These hand pies are best eaten the day they're made, as the crust tends to soften over time. But leftovers can be drizzled with icing and called breakfast danish. Just stir a cup of confectioner's sugar with a dribble of vanilla or almond extract and a splash of water until you get the right consistency for drizzling.

MAKES ABOUT A DOZEN, DEPENDING ON SIZE

For the crust:

2 cups all-purpose flour

1 tablespoon granulated sugar

1 teaspoon salt

1½ sticks (¾ cup) cold unsalted butter

4–6 tablespoons ice water

For the filling:

½ cup canned pumpkin or winter squash (if using fresh puree, drain well)

3 tablespoons light brown sugar, firmly packed

¼ teaspoon freshly squeezed lemon juice

⅛ teaspoon ground nutmeg

⅛ teaspoon ground ginger

⅛ teaspoon ground allspice

⅛ teaspoon salt

For the crust, mix the flour, sugar, and salt in food processor. Pulse briefly until combined. Add the cold butter and process 10–15 seconds until the butter pieces stop jumping around like popcorn. Through the feed tube, add 4 tablespoons (¼ cup) of the ice water (minus the ice cubes). Process 3–5 seconds until the liquid is well dispersed and the dough starts to clump a bit. Add more ice water 1 tablespoon at a time, processing a few seconds afterward, until the flour comes together into a dough around the sides of the bowl. You don't want it too wet, but if you squeeze a bit in your hand, it should hold together instead of falling apart into dry crumbles. (If you don't have a food processor, you can also work the butter into the dry ingredients with a stand mixer fitted with a paddle attachment, a pastry blender, or your fingers.)

Dump the dough onto the counter and form it into two equal balls. Flatten each ball into a disk less than 1 inch thick. Fold each disk in half, then in half again. Flatten the dough back down into a disk. Wrap the dough in plastic wrap, waxed paper, or a reusable wrap. Let the dough rest in the refrigerator for 20 minutes while you make the filling.

For the filling, stir together the pumpkin or squash puree, brown sugar, lemon juice, spices, and salt in a medium bowl until well combined.

Preheat the oven to 425°F. Grease or line two sheet pans with parchment paper.

For assembly:

1 large egg, for the egg wash

Coarse sugar for sprinkling (optional)

Remove one of the dough disks from the refrigerator and roll it out to ⅛ inch thick on a floured counter with a rolling pin. Cut out pumpkin shapes with cookie cutters or just cut out circles using a biscuit cutter, juice glass, or mason jar. (You can also cut out rectangles or squares to fold over like turnovers.) Press together the scraps and reroll until you use all the dough (if it gets hard to roll, wrap up the dough again and chill it for 20 minutes). To create jack-o'-lantern faces, it's best to freeze the dough in order to get clean cuts and minimize frustration. Arrange all of the cutouts from the first batch of dough on a sheet pan, and set them in the freezer for 20 minutes before proceeding.

In the meantime, roll out the second dough disk and cut it into the same-sized shapes—these will be the undecorated bottoms. Chill in the refrigerator while you finish the tops.

Once the dough in the freezer is firm, remove a few at a time, cutting out faces in various expressions (for best results, use a very sharp paring knife with a pointy tip). Return them to the freezer and repeat for the rest.

To assemble, pair up similarly sized shapes and place a tablespoon of filling (or more, depending on the size of your cutters) in the center of the undecorated bottoms, leaving a ¼-inch margin. Using a little bowl of water, wet a finger and moisten that edge all around the filling. Top it with a jack-o'-lantern face, pressing along the edges to seal and crimping with the floured tines of a fork. Repeat with the remaining filling and dough. If you're not cutting faces, be sure to cut out a few steam vents to prevent the pies from bursting.

Set the hand pies on the prepared pans. In a small bowl, beat the egg with a teaspoon of water and brush the egg wash over the tops of the pies, taking care not to smear the filling. Sprinkle with coarse sugar, if desired. Bake 18–20 minutes (depending on size) until the pies are a rich golden brown. Remove from the oven and let cool. Serve warm or room temperature on their own or with vanilla ice cream. Store leftovers in an airtight container for 3–4 days in the refrigerator.

Spiced Apple Layer Cake with Brown Butter Frosting

~~~~~~

This festive autumn apple cake will help you ring in the season in style. Apples, spiced with cinnamon and nutmeg, are nestled between layers of applesauce cake and finished with a freckled brown butter frosting. For best results, make the apple compote and brown the butter for the frosting the day before you want to serve the cake. Even the cake layers can be made a day in advance (just make sure they cool down completely, wrap them in plastic, and store them in their pans in the refrigerator). Then all that's left is the assembly. To prevent the butter from spitting and hissing while browning, let the butter come to room temperature first. Any leftover apple filling can be used to decorate the frosted cake or saved and layered with Greek yogurt and granola to make Apple Pie Parfaits.

SERVES 12–16

For the filling:

2 tablespoons unsalted butter

2½ pounds cooking apples (like Braeburn, Mutsu, Honeycrisp, Jonagold, or Granny Smith), peeled, cut into ¼- to ½-inch dice

1 cup apple cider

½ cup granulated sugar

1 tablespoon lemon juice, freshly squeezed

1 teaspoon ground cinnamon

¼ teaspoon ground nutmeg

Pinch of salt

1 tablespoon cornstarch

1 tablespoon cold water

For the brown butter:

1 stick (½ cup) unsalted butter, at cool room temperature

For the filling, melt the butter over medium heat in a large sauté pan. Add the diced apples, cider, sugar, lemon juice, cinnamon, nutmeg, and salt. Bring to a simmer and cook over medium-low heat, uncovered, stirring occasionally, for 10–14 minutes until the apples are tender (but not mushy). In a small bowl, whisk the cornstarch into the water until dissolved. Stir it into the apple mixture and continue cooking, stirring frequently, until thickened, about 1 minute. Let cool. Store covered in the refrigerator for up to 2 weeks.

For the brown butter, melt the butter in a small saucepan over medium-low heat. Continue cooking 5–10 minutes. The butter will bubble and the solids at the bottom of the pan will turn gold then start to brown quickly. Scrape the bottom of the pan with a wooden spoon frequently toward the end of the cooking time to loosen those caramelized solids and prevent them from burning. Remove the pan from the heat once the solids are a deep, dark brown and the butter itself is the color of medium- to dark-amber maple syrup. Transfer the brown butter to a bowl and place in the refrigerator until it starts to resolidify, but is still soft, 2–3 hours. (If it chills solid, just set it at room temperature for an hour or very gently rewarm in the microwave in 5- to 10-second increments until soft but not melted.)

For the cake:

2¼ cups all-purpose flour

2 teaspoons baking powder

¼ teaspoon baking soda

1 teaspoon ground cinnamon

½ teaspoon ground allspice

¼ teaspoon salt

1 stick (½ cup) unsalted butter, at room temperature

1¼ cups light brown sugar, firmly packed

3 large eggs, at room temperature

2 teaspoons vanilla extract

½ cup unsweetened applesauce

For the frosting:

1 stick (½ cup) unsalted butter, at cool room temperature

2 cups confectioner's sugar, sifted

1 teaspoon lemon juice, freshly squeezed

Pinch of salt

Preheat the oven to 375°F. Grease two 8- or 9-inch round cake pans and line them with circles of parchment paper.

For the cake, sift together the flour, baking powder, baking soda, spices, and salt in a medium bowl. Set aside.

Beat the butter for 1 minute on medium speed until creamy. Scrape down the bottom and sides of the bowl and add the brown sugar. Beat 2–3 minutes on medium-high speed until very fluffy. Scraping down the bottom and sides of the bowl as needed, add the eggs, one at a time, beating on medium-high for 1 minute after each addition. Mix in the vanilla. (If the batter should start to break, mix on medium-high until it comes back together.)

Add ⅓ of the dry ingredients to the batter and mix on low until combined. With the mixer running, slowly pour in half the applesauce. Add half of the remaining dry ingredients and mix on low until combined, scraping down the bottom and sides of the bowl as needed. With the mixer running on low speed, slowly add the rest of the applesauce until combined. Mix in the rest of the dry ingredients.

Divide the batter equally into the two prepared pans, spreading evenly. Bake 18–22 minutes, rotating the pans halfway through baking, until a toothpick inserted into the center of the cakes comes out clean. Let cool completely.

For the frosting, combine the cool room temperature butter with the brown butter in the bowl of an electric mixer, preferably fitted with the paddle attachment. Beat on medium speed until smooth. Scraping down the bottom and sides of the bowl as needed, add the confectioner's sugar in two batches, beating on low after each addition. Add the salt and half the lemon juice. Beat well on medium speed. Taste and add the remaining lemon juice, if desired. If the frosting is too soft, chill in the refrigerator 20 minutes before assembling.

To assemble the cake, remove the cake layers from their pans and peel off the parchment paper rounds. Arrange one of the layers right-side-up on a serving plate or pedestal. Spread the spiced apple compote on top, leaving a ½ inch perimeter around the edge, and reserving ¼–½ cup of the compote to decorate the top, if desired. Arrange the second cake layer upside-down on top of the apple compote. Pipe or spread frosting into the gap between the cake layers to seal in the apple compote (an easy way to do this is to scoop ⅓ of the frosting into a resealable sandwich bag, zip it tight, snip one of the bottom corners, and squeeze the frosting into the gap all the way around). Frost the sides, then the top of the cake. If you like, you can spoon the remaining apple compote around the outer edge of the cake, letting the sauce drip down the sides.

Serve the cake at room temperature so the frosting is soft. Store leftovers covered in the refrigerator for 2–3 days. Take the cake out an hour or so before serving to let the frosting come to room temperature.

Classic Apple Pie

Cinnamon is the quintessential autumn spice. But, for me, no apple pie is complete without nutmeg. This long-baked pie is deeply comforting. I also like to add a touch of apple cider vinegar to the crust. The raw dough may smell strongly of vinegar, but don't worry, once cooked it creates a delightfully flaky and flavorful crust. Serve this pie with a scoop of Connecticut Valley Vanilla Ice Cream or, for a true New England experience, a few slices of sharp cheddar cheese on the side, such as Cabot Clothbound or Seriously Sharp.

SERVES 8–12

For the crust:

2 cups all-purpose flour

1 tablespoon granulated sugar

1 teaspoon salt

1½ sticks (¾ cup) cold unsalted butter, cut into 12 pieces

1 tablespoon apple cider vinegar

4–6 tablespoons ice water

For the filling:

3 pounds mixed apples (about 6–8 medium), like Northern Spy, Rhode Island Greening, Granny Smith, or Cortland

1 tablespoon freshly squeezed lemon juice (about ½ lemon)

2 tablespoons all-purpose flour

¾ cup light brown sugar, firmly packed

1 teaspoon ground cinnamon

½ teaspoon ground nutmeg

For the crust, mix the flour, sugar, and salt in a food processor. Pulse briefly until combined. Add the cold butter and process about 10 seconds until the butter pieces stop jumping around like popcorn. Through the feed tube, pour in the vinegar and ¼ cup of ice water (minus the ice cubes). Process until the liquid is well dispersed and the dough starts to clump a bit. If needed, add 1 or 2 more tablespoons of ice water, processing a few seconds each time, until the flour comes together into a dough around the sides of the bowl. If you squeeze a bit in your hand, it should hold together instead of falling apart into dry crumbles. (If you don't have a food processor, you can also work the butter into the dry ingredients with a stand mixer fitted with a paddle attachment, a pastry blender, or your fingers.)

Dump the dough onto the counter and bring it together, kneading gently once or twice to form layers. Form it into two balls, one slightly larger than the other. Flatten each into a disk less than 1 inch thick. Wrap them in plastic wrap, waxed paper, or a reusable wrap. Let them rest in the refrigerator for 30 minutes.

Meanwhile, peel, core, and slice the apples thinly and place in a large bowl. Stir in the lemon juice and dust with the flour, tossing once or twice. Add the sugar, cinnamon, and nutmeg.

Preheat the oven to 400°F. Remove the dough from the refrigerator. Flour your counter and rolling pin well. The dough shouldn't stick at all. Take the larger dough disk and roll it out about ¼ inch thick, about 12 inches in diameter.

For preparation:

1 egg, beaten

1 teaspoon water

Roll from the middle out in all directions. Don't grind the dough down into the counter—push it out to the sides. If the dough sticks, and it may, sprinkle more flour. Transfer to a 9-inch pie dish by lifting the edge of the dough over the top of the rolling pin (I use a bench scraper for this, but you could also use a spatula). Gently lift and push until the dough is draped over the rolling pin. Align the dough over the pie plate so it's centered and gently unfurl.

Pour the apple mixture into the dough-lined pie plate. Roll out the second crust the same way, only slightly smaller, and drape the second crust over the fruit. Fold the edges of the top crust over and under the edges of the bottom crust and flute decoratively, if desired. Cut steam vents on the top with a sharp paring knife. In a small bowl, beat the egg and water with a fork. Brush the dough with the egg wash.

Place the pie plate on a baking sheet and bake for 20 minutes at 400°F. Reduce the heat to 350°F and bake until the crust is golden brown and the juices are bubbly, 45–55 minutes more. If the crust is getting too brown, set a sheet of aluminum foil over the top.

Remove the pie from the oven and let cool for 20 minutes. Serve warm with vanilla or buttermilk ice cream. Homemade pie crusts are always best the day they're made, but any remaining pie can be stored, loosely covered, at room temperature or in the refrigerator for 3 days. It also makes a terrific breakfast.

Maple Walnut Pie

Consider this New England's answer to Southern pecan pie. English walnuts pair well with local maple syrup and toasty brown butter. Cornmeal adds texture to the filling. Tangy cream cheese in the crust helps to counter some of the sweetness. Still, this pie is very sweet and decadent. It makes a great addition to your Thanksgiving dessert repertoire. Feel free to add in other nuts, like local butternuts, shagbark hickory nuts, or black walnuts. Just be advised that black walnuts have a much stronger, almost pungent flavor that may take you by surprise if you've never tried them before. Taste one first before deciding whether to commit to a whole pie.

SERVES 12–16

For the crust:

1 cup all-purpose flour

1 stick (½ cup) unsalted butter, cut into 8 pieces

3 ounces cream cheese, cut into 3 pieces

½ teaspoon salt

For the filling:

1 stick (½ cup) unsalted butter, at cool room temperature

¾ cup light brown sugar, firmly packed

¼ cup fine yellow cornmeal

½ teaspoon kosher salt

½ cup maple syrup (the darker, the better)

¼ cup heavy cream

½ teaspoon vanilla extract

4 egg yolks

1½ cups shelled walnut pieces

Preheat the oven to 350°F. Set aside a 9-inch pie plate.

For the crust, add the flour, butter, cream cheese, and salt to the bowl of a food processor, and process until it starts to clump together, 10–20 seconds. Turn the dough onto a sheet of waxed paper, plastic wrap, or reusable wrap. Gather it into a flat disk, fold it in half, then in half again, and reflatten into a disk. (If you don't have a food processor, you can also work the butter into the dry ingredients with a stand mixer fitted with a paddle attachment, a pastry blender, or your fingers.) Wrap the dough and refrigerate for 30 minutes.

For the filling, melt the butter in a small pot over medium-low heat. Continue cooking 5–10 minutes. The butter will bubble and the solids at the bottom of the pan will turn gold then start to brown quickly. Scrape the bottom of the pan with a wooden spoon frequently toward the end of the cooking time to loosen those caramelized solids and prevent them from burning. Remove the pan from the heat once the solids are a deep, dark brown and the butter itself is the color of medium- to dark-amber maple syrup.

Whisk the brown sugar, cornmeal, and salt in a medium bowl until well mixed. Add the brown butter and maple syrup. Beat with a wooden spoon until combined. Add the cream and vanilla. Beat 1 minute more. Add the egg yolks, and mix just until homogenous.

Remove the dough from the refrigerator and roll out on a floured counter or between sheets of waxed paper about ¼ inch thick or thinner, and 12 inches in diameter. Transfer to a 9-inch pie plate, fluting the edges if desired. Spread the nuts evenly in the pie shell. Pour the filling over the nuts.

Bake the pie 40–50 minutes on the middle rack until the crust is a deep golden brown. The filling will still look dangerously loose when jiggled, but it will set once cool. If you're worried, leave it in the oven an extra 5 minutes (you can cover the crust with foil to prevent it from burning). Let cool at room temperature and then refrigerate for at least 4 hours. Serve with a dollop of unsweetened whipped cream.

Eastham Turnip Snacking Cake with Crème Fraîche Glaze

I know what you're thinking: Turnips? But, listen, nobody bats an eye at carrots or zucchini or pumpkin in dessert. In fact, I love turnips, especially the sweet Eastham variety grown on Cape Cod, as well as Westport's (MA) Macomber turnip. But, really, any ordinary, purple-topped turnip or rutabaga will do. I can assure you, this cake is delicious. You can either keep it simple and dust the top with confectioner's sugar or ice with sweetened crème fraîche, which puts it squarely into carrot cake territory—and yet uniquely apart. Look for crème fraîche that's very thick (you could also substitute sour cream).

SERVES 9–12

For the cake:

1 medium turnip (at least ¼ pound), peeled, cut into 2-inch chunks

1½ sticks (¾ cup) unsalted butter, at cool room temperature

1¼ cups light brown sugar, firmly packed

3 large eggs, at room temperature

1 teaspoon vanilla extract

1 cup all-purpose flour, divided

1½ teaspoons baking powder

½ teaspoon ground nutmeg

¼ teaspoon salt

For the glaze:

½ cup crème fraîche (like Vermont Creamery)

1½ cups confectioner's sugar, sifted

In a pot of boiling water, cook the turnip chunks until tender enough to pierce with a fork, about 20 minutes. Drain well. Either mash very well with a potato masher or puree in a food processor until it's the texture of applesauce. Measure out ½ cup of turnip puree and set aside.

Preheat the oven to 350°F. Grease an 8 × 8-inch baking pan.

With an electric mixer (preferably fitted with a paddle attachment), beat the butter and brown sugar until fluffy, starting on low speed and building up to medium-high, 2–3 minutes. Scrape down the bottom and sides of the bowl as needed. Add the eggs, one at a time, beating well after each addition. Mix in the vanilla. Add half of the flour and all of the baking powder, nutmeg, and salt. Mix on low just until combined. Add the turnip and the rest of the flour, and continue mixing on low until combined. Pour the batter into the prepared pan, spreading evenly.

Bake 30–35 minutes until the top is deeply golden brown, the cake is set through the middle, and a toothpick inserted into the center comes out clean. Let cool completely.

For the glaze, whisk the confectioner's sugar into the crème fraîche a little at a time until smooth. (You may need more or less sugar depending on how thick your crème fraîche is and how sweet you like your icing.) Spread the glaze over the cooled cake. Grate some fresh nutmeg on top if desired. The cake can be stored, covered, in the refrigerator 3–4 days.

Apple Raspberry Crisp

Apple-picking is a favorite autumn tradition across New England. Even more fun than selecting the perfect apple, twisting the fruit off the branch, and biting into its crisp, bracing tartness is creating a menu of all the potential desserts your bounty will create in the months ahead. I love the burst of color and flavor that raspberries bring to a traditional apple crisp. I like to use a mix of apples for a more rounded, well-balanced flavor, which is good because I can never keep track of the mixed-up jumble of apple varieties in my pick-your-own bag.

SERVES 6–8

For the topping:

½ cup all-purpose flour

⅓ cup light brown sugar, firmly packed

5 tablespoons cold unsalted butter, cut into ½-inch cubes

¼ teaspoon salt

½ teaspoon vanilla extract

¾ cup rolled oats

For the filling:

6–8 assorted apples (like Northern Spy, Granny Smith, and Cortland), peeled, cored, cut into ¼-inch thick slices

⅓ cup raspberries

⅓ cup granulated sugar

2 tablespoons all-purpose flour

1 teaspoon freshly squeezed lemon juice

1 teaspoon ground cinnamon

Preheat the oven to 350°F. Liberally butter an 8 × 8-inch baking dish or 9-inch deep-dish pie plate.

For the topping, combine the flour, brown sugar, butter, salt, and vanilla extract in a food processor. Pulse until crumbly, with butter pieces the size of small peas. (You can also work the butter into the dry ingredients in a medium bowl with your fingers.) Stir in the oats.

In a large bowl, combine the sliced apples, raspberries, sugar, flour, lemon juice, and cinnamon. Spread evenly in the baking dish. Remove the processor blade and pour the topping over the fruit, distributing well.

Bake 50–55 minutes, until the apples are tender and bubbling and the top is golden brown (use the broiler at the end if you must). Serve warm with Connecticut Valley Vanilla Ice Cream or Maine Buttermilk and Sea Salt Ice Cream. Leftovers can be stored, covered, in the refrigerator and reheated in the oven.

Pear Cranberry Slab Pie

When you need pie for a crowd, that's when you ditch the pie plate and pull out the 9 × 13-inch pan. From there, you can cut the pie into neat slabs rather than messy slices. Here the sweet pears tame the tartness of the cranberries, while the red berries add festive color. The trick is getting your pears to ripen in time for the big event. Bartlett and Anjou pears usually ripen in 3–5 days at room temperature, while Boscs takes more like 5–7. Try keeping them in a paper bag with a ripe apple or banana to speed up the process (if they ripen too soon, the pears will hold in the refrigerator). But if your pears are still rock hard, you can substitute apples with good results (just add an extra ¼ cup of sugar). The long, slow baking time will reward you with a crisp, deeply flavored crust.

MAKES 1 9 × 13-INCH PIE OR
2 STANDARD 9-INCH PIES
SERVING 16–24

For the crust:

4 cups all-purpose flour

2 tablespoons granulated sugar

2 teaspoons kosher salt

3 sticks (1½ cups) cold unsalted butter, each stick cut into 8 pieces

½–¾ cup ice water

For the filling:

3 pounds pears, peeled, cored, thinly sliced (about 8–9 medium pears)

1 cup cranberries (or more)

½ cup granulated sugar

2 tablespoons cornstarch

1 teaspoon ground cinnamon

¼ teaspoon ground nutmeg

⅛ teaspoon ground allspice

For the crust, mix the flour, sugar, and salt in a large food processor. Pulse briefly until combined. Add the cold butter and process about 20 seconds until the butter pieces stop jumping around like popcorn and incorporate into the flour. Remove the top and use a butter knife to stir up any large pieces of butter. If they're bigger than pea-sized, process a few seconds longer. Through the feed tube, pour in ½ cup of ice water (minus the ice cubes). Process 5 seconds until the liquid is well dispersed and the dough starts to clump a bit. Add more ice water 1 tablespoon at a time, processing a few seconds afterward, until the flour comes together into a dough around the sides of the bowl. You don't want it too wet, but if you squeeze a bit in your hand, it should hold together instead of falling apart into dry crumbles. (If you don't have a food processor, you can also cut the butter into the dry ingredients with a stand mixer fitted with a paddle attachment, a pastry blender, or your fingers.)

Dump the dough onto the counter and form it into two balls, one twice as large as the other. Fold each dough ball over on itself once or twice to create layers. Flatten each ball into a disk less than 1 inch thick. Wrap them in plastic wrap, waxed paper, or a reusable wrap. Let them rest in the refrigerator for half an hour.

Preheat the oven to 375°F. Butter a 9 × 13-inch rectangular baking pan (or 2 standard 9-inch pie plates).

For the egg wash:

1 large egg, beaten

1 tablespoon water

1 teaspoon granulated sugar

In a large bowl, combine the sliced pears, cranberries, sugar, cornstarch, and spices.

Between 2 large sheets of parchment paper, roll out the larger dough disk ⅛ inch thick to a rectangle with dimensions of at least 13 × 17 inches. Peel off one sheet of the parchment. Invert the dough over the baking pan (centered), parchment-side-up. Gently peel off the paper. Arrange the dough in the pan without stretching it, nudging it into the corners and letting the excess hang over the sides. Pour the filling over the dough and spread evenly. Trim the overhanging dough and fold it over so it rests on the filling.

Roll out the second smaller dough disk to ¼ inch thick. Using decorative cookie cutters, circular biscuit cutters, or a small glass, cut out shapes and lay them all over the filling, overlapping in some areas and leaving some filling uncovered (you could also do a lattice top).

In a small bowl, beat the egg and water together with a fork until well blended. Brush the top crust with the egg wash and sprinkle with sugar.

Bake the pie on the middle rack for 45 minutes at 375°F. Then reduce the heat to 325°F for 35–45 more minutes. This will ensure that the filling isn't runny and the crust gets deeply browned. (If the crust starts to burn, lay a sheet of aluminum foil on top.) Let cool 20 minutes. Serve warm or room temperature with a scoop of Connecticut Valley Vanilla Ice Cream or Maine Buttermilk and Sea Salt Ice Cream. Cover leftovers loosely with foil and store at room temperature or in the refrigerator for up to 3 days.

Winter

*W*inter in New England has a tranquil beauty all its own. Lush mounds of snow drape the towering evergreens while the spare silhouettes of the bare hardwoods have a sculptural quality. Deep snowfall cushions the landscape in a soft, muffled silence, the only sound the cottony squeak of boots pressed into snow. When a nor'easter inevitably blows through, a slushy mix of freezing rain glazes everything, branches to rooflines, in sparkling glass. Barns, covered bridges, and weathered old saltboxes are rimmed with icy stalactites. Even the local gas station looks briefly charming. For a moment, the world is frozen into a winter wonderland. That is, until reality sets in and I reluctantly head outside to shovel my car out of a roadside snowbank.

It's time to break out the puffy coats, wool socks, and ski gloves. Me, I've had them on since mid-October, since my metabolism could best be described as hypothermic. But I do appreciate the brisk, bracing air that shocks me into a more lively, energetic state of consciousness. I find you're never too old to reacquaint yourself with the miracle of snowflakes. Children build snow forts, sled ramps, and snow people complete with beloved family pets. Frozen ponds beckon bladed feet to the slick, icy surface to carve graceful arcs and whooping, high-velocity etchings that spray ice shavings in a flurry. And while skiers and snowboarders take to the slopes, the less sporty among us might head to the kitchen, where cozying up to the oven offers respite from stress and the elements.

It's time to embrace all the flavors of a New England winter: dried fruits, nuts, caramel, butterscotch, chocolate, spices, and rum. This chapter offers plenty of classic cookie and candy recipes to charm family and friends, from homey Snickerdoodles (page 146) to elegantly rustic Rosemary Juniper Shortbread (page 164). It offers several flavors of homemade fudge and Maine Potato Candy (page 181) (don't knock it 'til you try it). There are show-stopping holiday desserts, like the Cranberry Swirl Cheesecake (page 153), as well as an array of cozy puddings to keep you warm all winter long, including Butterscotch (page 150), Tapioca (page 169), and Cornmeal Molasses (page 157) (the dessert formerly known as Indian pudding).

While there isn't much coming out of the New England fields in the wintertime, you can still eat seasonally and locally by stocking up on autumn-harvested crops. Apples and pears can hold for months under cool, dry conditions. Same for winter squashes, root vegetables, potatoes, and nuts. Once the steam starts billowing from the hillside sugar shacks in late February and March, that's the sign that winter is winding down and the natural cycle begins once again.

Nuts

English walnuts are often the first nuts that come to mind when we think of New England desserts, but those aren't the only nuts to consider in your baking exploits. Several types of native nuts grow wild throughout New England, including hickory, hazelnut, chestnut, butternut, and black walnuts (the latter have a much stronger—some might say "acquired"—taste). The Native Peoples used all of these nuts in their cooking. If you find some, consider using them in any recipe that calls for nuts, like Butter Nut Snowballs (page 159) and Maple Walnut Pie (page 135), New England's answer to Southern pecan pie.

Dried Fruits

Drying fruit is a brilliantly inventive and energy-efficient way to preserve warm weather harvests through the off-season. Removing the water prevents spoilage, while the fruit retains most of the nutrients. The resulting chew and concentrated sweetness are a boon to baked goods. Raisins and dried currants add flavor and texture to Rum Raisin Oatmeal Cookies (page 147) and old-fashioned Hermits (page 155). Dried cranberries provide tartness and color to Cranberry Pine Nut Biscotti (page 179). And dates lend sweetness and moisture to the Spicy Gingerbread (page 149).

Snickerdoodles

This is a classic New England cookie—crisp on the outside, soft on the inside, and flavored with cinnamon sugar. It's so simple yet so crowd-pleasing. Tracking down the origins of the funny name has been tricky. One plausible theory is that they're an American adaptation of Schneckennudeln, a type of cinnamon roll that was brought over by German immigrants. Whatever their origin, these cookies are much beloved all over New England. I've adapted this recipe from my mother-in-law, Jean, who was born and bred in Massachusetts and has a wicked Boston accent to prove it. Cream of tartar (a white acidic powder found in the spice aisle) creates the signature flavor and acidity that, together with baking soda, enables the cookies to rise—so don't leave it out.

MAKES ABOUT 3 DOZEN

2 sticks (1 cup) unsalted butter, at cool room temperature

1½ cups granulated sugar

2 large eggs, at room temperature

2¾ cups all-purpose flour

2 teaspoons cream of tartar

1 teaspoon baking soda

½ teaspoon table salt

For the sugar mixture:

2 tablespoons granulated sugar

1½ teaspoons ground cinnamon

Preheat the oven to 400°F. Grease or line two cookie sheets with parchment paper.

With an electric mixer (preferably fitted with a paddle attachment), cream the butter and sugar together on medium speed for 1–2 minutes. Scrape down the sides and bottom of the bowl with a spatula as needed. Add the eggs, one at a time, mixing well after each addition. Continue beating 2–3 minutes on medium until very fluffy.

In a medium bowl, sift together the flour, cream of tartar, baking soda, and salt. Add the dry ingredients to the butter mixture. Mix on low, scraping down the sides and bottom of the bowl at least once, until the mixture comes together into a soft dough.

In a small bowl, stir together the sugar and cinnamon until well combined. Using a ½-ounce cookie scoop or tablespoon, portion out the dough into small balls about 1¼ inches in diameter. Roll each between your hands until smoothed. Drop them, one at a time, into the bowl of cinnamon-sugar and swirl until coated. Place the dough balls 3 inches apart on the prepared pan, 12 to a sheet.

Bake 8–10 minutes until puffed and just starting to crack. The sides will be set but the tops will still be soft. Remove the cookies from the oven and let them sit on the hot pan for 3 more minutes before transferring them to racks to cool. Fully cooled cookies may be stored in an airtight container for 5–6 days.

Rum Raisin Oatmeal Cookies

I feel like I'm one of the last holdouts who still prefers raisins in their oatmeal cookies instead of chocolate chips. My beloved oatmeal raisin cookies are a dying breed, so I knew I had to include a recipe for these homely stalwarts of ye olde New England. And while all the kids are standing on the other side of the room, why not add a splash of rum? Feel free to increase the rum to your taste, decreasing the amount of water by the same amount so your total liquid is ¼ cup. If, like the rest of my family, your hatred of raisins eclipses your love of cookies, you are, of course, entitled to omit them and add a cup of chocolate chips. Me, I'll be off in the other room hoarding the last of my oatmeal raisin cookies like a raccoon on trash day.

MAKES ABOUT 30

1 cup raisins

2 tablespoons dark rum

2 tablespoons water

2 sticks (1 cup) unsalted butter, at cool room temperature

1 cup light brown sugar, firmly packed

½ cup granulated sugar

2 large eggs, at room temperature

2 teaspoons vanilla extract

1½ cups all-purpose flour

½ teaspoon baking soda

½ teaspoon baking powder

1 teaspoon table salt

1 teaspoon ground cinnamon

¼ teaspoon ground nutmeg

3 cups rolled oats (not instant)

Preheat the oven to 350°F. Grease or line two cookie sheets with parchment paper.

Add the raisins, rum, and water to a small saucepan and cover with a lid. Bring to a simmer over medium heat (check often so they don't burn). Remove from the heat, take off the lid, and stir. The raisins will plump and absorb most of the liquid. Let cool while making the cookie dough.

With an electric mixer (preferably fitted with a paddle attachment), cream the butter for 1 minute on medium speed. Scraping down the bottom and sides of the bowl as needed, add the sugars and beat 2–3 minutes, starting on low and gradually increasing the speed to medium-high, until very fluffy. Add the eggs, one at a time, beating well after each addition. Dribble in the vanilla and mix again. Add the flour, baking soda, baking powder, salt, and spices. Mix on low until just starting to come together. Add the oats to the bowl followed by the raisins and any residual rum. Mix on low for about 30 seconds until the raisins are well dispersed.

Drop the dough in heaping tablespoons or a 1-ounce cookie scoop spaced 2 inches apart on the prepared pan, 12 per pan (with some extra dough for a partial third pan).

Bake 12–15 minutes until golden on the edges and a little on top, and the centers are still soft when gently pressed. Let sit on the hot pan 5 minutes before transferring to a rack to cool. Store cooled cookies in an airtight container 4–5 days.

Spicy Gingerbread

Come holiday time, I get a hankering for gingerbread. This one gets its kick from a double dose of ginger—dried and freshly grated—as well as cinnamon and cloves. If you prefer your gingerbread on the tamer side, feel free to reduce the fresh ginger to 1 tablespoon instead of 2. It will still be plenty flavorful. In the spirit of Sticky Toffee Pudding, I added dates in addition to molasses to balance the flavor and keep the cake fluffy and moist instead of heavy and dense. All it needs is some lightly sweetened whipped cream to ring in the festivities.

SERVES 12–16

- 3 ounces Medjool dates (about 5), pitted
- ½ cup water
- 2 large eggs, at room temperature
- ½ cup molasses
- ¼ cup light brown sugar, firmly packed
- 2 tablespoons peeled and finely grated fresh ginger (a microplane grater works best)
- 1 teaspoon vanilla extract
- 1½ cups all-purpose flour
- 1 teaspoon baking soda
- ½ teaspoon baking powder
- 1 teaspoon ground ginger
- ½ teaspoon ground cinnamon
- ¼ teaspoon ground cloves
- ½ teaspoon table salt
- ½ cup buttermilk, well shaken
- 1 stick (½ cup) unsalted butter, melted

Preheat the oven to 325°F. Grease an 8 × 8-inch baking pan.

Combine the pitted dates and water in a small saucepan and bring to a simmer. Remove the pan from the heat and let sit covered for 10–15 minutes while preparing the other ingredients.

Beat the eggs in a large bowl. Add the molasses, brown sugar, grated fresh ginger, and vanilla. Whisk well.

In a medium bowl, whisk together the flour, baking soda, baking powder, spices, and salt.

Puree the dates together with the soaking water in a food processor. Set aside.

Add half of the dry ingredients to the egg mixture and beat with a wooden spoon just until combined. Gradually stir in the buttermilk. Add the rest of the dry ingredients and stir until combined. Add the pureed dates and melted butter. Beat well. Pour the batter into the prepared pan.

Bake 40–45 minutes until a toothpick inserted into the center comes out with only moist crumbs attached (no raw batter). Let cool.

Serve warm or room temperature with lightly sweetened whipped cream. Store covered at room temperature for 4–5 days, or in the refrigerator for 1 week.

Butterscotch Pudding

In my version of this cozy pudding, butter and dark brown sugar are cooked just long enough to create a cascade of flavorful Maillard reactions, boosted by vanilla and a generous sprinkling of sea salt. Contrary to popular belief, butterscotch does not traditionally contain Scotch whiskey (though you're welcome to add some to cut the sweetness).

SERVES 6–8

4 cups whole milk

¼ cup cornstarch

1 teaspoon kosher or sea salt

1 stick (½ cup) unsalted butter

1½ cups dark brown sugar, firmly packed

4 large egg yolks

1 cup heavy cream

2 teaspoons vanilla

Flaky sea salt to serve

Heat the milk in the microwave for 2 minutes on high to warm. In a small bowl, whisk the cornstarch, salt, and about ½ cup of the warm milk until smooth. Whisk it into the rest of the milk and set aside.

Melt the butter in a medium pot over medium-low heat. Add the brown sugar and cook, stirring constantly with a wooden spoon, 3–5 minutes. The mixture will start out dark and wet, but, once it starts bubbling, it will start to lighten in color, thicken, and become almost dry around the edges. Keep stirring, digging the wooden spoon into the corner edges of the pot, until the entire mixture is light, thick, and smells deeply butterscotchy.

Slowly whisk in the warm milk in a steady stream. Once you've gotten about half the milk in, add the rest all at once. Increase the heat to medium and bring to a boil, whisking often until the mixture thickens and coats the back of a spoon, about 5 minutes more. Remove from the heat.

In a medium bowl, whisk the yolks together with the cream. Temper the egg mixture by slowly drizzling 1 cup of the hot milk mixture into the egg yolk mixture, whisking vigorously. Then whisk the tempered egg mixture back into the pot and return to medium-low heat. Cook 2–3 minutes, whisking constantly, until steamy and just shy of simmering (if you accidentally bring it to a boil, you can strain the finished mixture to remove any coagulated egg yolk).

Remove from the heat and stir in the vanilla. Pour into individual jars or bowls, and tap them once or twice on the counter to pop any bubbles. To prevent a skin from forming, cover with plastic wrap set right against the surface of the pudding. Let cool in the refrigerator for at least 4–6 hours. To serve, top with a pinch of flaky sea salt.

Cranberry Swirl Cheesecake

This striking dessert is perfect for holiday get-togethers. The tartness of the cranberry topping cuts through the richness of the cheesecake. I've included a modified water bath for this recipe because otherwise the top tends to crack right along the beautiful swirly pattern. Setting a roasting pan with some water in the bottom of the oven helps to prevent cracking and creates a very light and custardy cheesecake. I've opted to use Biscoff Lotus cookies for the crust, a type of Belgian spice biscuit usually found in the specialty cookie aisle of the grocery store, but you could substitute traditional graham crackers with a shake or two of cinnamon in addition to the other spices. If you don't have Port for the cranberry swirl, you can use brandy. To keep it alcohol-free, just replace the Port with water.

SERVES 12–16

For the cranberry swirl:

1 cup fresh or frozen cranberries

¼ cup granulated sugar

¼ cup Ruby Port

½ cup apple cider or water

For the crust:

1½ cups (6 ounces) crushed Biscoff Lotus cookies

½ teaspoon ground allspice

⅛ teaspoon ground cloves

4 tablespoons unsalted butter, melted

For the filling:

4 (8-ounce) packages cream cheese (not low-fat), at room temperature

1 cup granulated sugar

Zest of 1 lemon (about ½ teaspoon)

4 large eggs, at room temperature

Preheat the oven to 325°F. Grease a 9-inch springform pan with butter.

For the cranberry swirl, combine all the ingredients in a small saucepan and bring to a boil over medium-high heat, stirring occasionally. Reduce the heat to medium-low and continue to simmer for 5–8 minutes or until all the cranberries have split their skins (if you're not sure, err on the side of cooking longer). Let cool. Run the mixture through a food processor or stick blender until smooth.

For the crust, grind the Biscoff cookies in a food processor until finely ground. Mix the cookie crumbs with the spices and melted butter. Press into the bottom of the prepared pan. Bake 5 minutes.

Wash and dry the bowl of the food processor well. Add the cream cheese and sugar. Process until smooth, about 1 minute. Scrape down the bottom and sides of the bowl with a rubber scraper. Add the lemon zest and all the eggs. Process until no lumps remain, 20–30 seconds. (You can also use an electric mixer, preferably fitted with a paddle attachment.)

Pour half of the filling over the crust and smooth the top. With a small spoon, add 10–20 dollops of cranberry sauce on top, sort of stabbing the spoon down into the filling about ½ inch several times to create each well. Spoon the rest of the batter on top (gently so the cranberry sauce doesn't spread), and smooth the top. Repeat with 15–20 more dollops of cranberry sauce (you may not use it all). Swirl the topping decoratively with the tip of a knife (don't over-swirl or the topping will disappear).

Reduce the oven temperature to 275°F. Place a roasting pan with ½ inch of water on the bottom rack to prevent cracking. Set the cheesecake on the middle rack and bake 1 hour. Turn the oven off, and let the cheesecake sit in the oven with the door *closed* for 1½–2 hours until cool.

Remove from the oven and let cool to room temperature. Chill in the refrigerator at least 6 hours or overnight before serving. Pass any remaining cranberry sauce at the table, if desired.

Hermits

These old-fashioned New England spice cookies get better with age, their flavor deepening by the day in an airtight container. This recipe is adapted from Wright's Dairy Farm & Bakery in North Smithfield, Rhode Island. Their hermits have a passionate cult following, which hopefully will soon include you. For mail orders, visit their website (wrightsdairyfarm.com).

MAKES ABOUT 2 DOZEN

1 cup raisins

2¾ cups all-purpose flour

½ teaspoon baking soda

½ teaspoon salt

1 teaspoon ground cinnamon

¼ teaspoon ground ginger

¼ teaspoon ground cloves

4 tablespoons unsalted butter, at cool room temperature

½ cup granulated sugar

½ cup molasses

1 large egg, at room temperature, plus 1 beaten egg white to brush on top

Preheat the oven to 375°F. Grease or line 2 cookie sheets with parchment paper.

In a small bowl, cover the raisins with 1 cup warm water and let soak for 10 minutes. In a medium bowl, whisk together the flour, baking soda, salt, and spices.

In a large bowl, cream together the butter and sugar with an electric mixer on medium-high speed until fluffy, 1–2 minutes. Scrape down the bottom and sides of the bowl with a rubber spatula as needed. Add the molasses and mix well, about 1 minute. Beat in the egg until smooth, 1–2 minutes.

Drain the raisins, reserving the soaking water. Measure out ¼ cup of the soaking water and discard the rest.

Add half of the dry ingredients to the sugar mixture, and mix on low speed just until combined. Add the raisins and mix on low until well-dispersed. Add the ¼ cup soaking water to the mixture along with the remaining dry ingredients. Mix on low just until blended.

Divide the soft dough into quarters. On each pan, form two logs about 12 inches long and 1½ inches wide. Set each log about 3 inches apart to account for spread. (I find it easiest to use a small cookie scoop to create 6 or 7 mounds in a row and then press or smear them together with a rubber spatula.) Flatten the logs to ¼–⅓ inches high. Brush the tops with beaten egg white.

Bake 15–18 minutes until the edges are set but the centers are still soft (you want them slightly underbaked in the middle). Remove from the oven, let cool on the pan, and cut each loaf into 6 bars. Store the cooled cookies in an airtight container for up to 2 weeks.

Cornmeal Molasses Pudding

This corn-based pudding, traditionally known as Indian pudding, is made all across New England. Flavored with molasses and spice, it's incredibly warm and delicious on a cold night with vanilla ice cream. Another benefit: it's gluten-free. I've opted to use a slow-cooker instead of a water bath in the oven because it's a little more user-friendly, but the occasional stirring that's required means it can't be left entirely unattended. Since everyone's slow-cooker is slightly different, times are merely suggestions. Rely on visual cues instead.

SERVES 8–12

- 4 tablespoons unsalted butter
- 6 cups milk (preferably whole, but not skim), divided
- ½ cup molasses
- 2 large eggs
- 1 cup yellow cornmeal
- ¼ cup granulated sugar
- 1 teaspoon kosher salt
- 1 teaspoon ground cinnamon
- 1 teaspoon ground ginger
- ¼ teaspoon ground nutmeg

Melt the butter in the microwave or a small pot on the stove. Pour it into the bowl of a 4- to 8-quart slow-cooker. Heat 3 cups of milk in the microwave or on the stove until warmed. Add the milk to the slow-cooker. Whisk in the molasses.

In a medium bowl, whisk the eggs well before whisking them into the milk mixture. Whisk in the cornmeal, sugar, salt, cinnamon, ginger, and nutmeg.

Cover the slow-cooker and set big, oval 7- to 8-quart pots to low and smaller, round 4- to 6-quart pots to high. Cook until bubbling around the edges (30–60 minutes), stirring every 30 minutes. Make sure to get into the corners of the pot with a sturdy wooden spoon and whisk to remove any lumps.

Once bubbling, heat the remaining 3 cups of milk until warm and stir it into the slow-cooker. Continue cooking, whisking every half hour, until thickened to the consistency of a thick porridge, for a total cooking time of 2–3 hours.

Let cool slightly and serve warm right from the crock with vanilla ice cream. To store, remove the crock from the electric base and set it on the stove until cool enough to handle. Cover with plastic wrap set right over the surface to prevent a rubbery skin from forming (cut a few steam vents with a sharp paring knife). Store, covered, in the refrigerator for up to 1 week. To reheat, gently warm in the microwave.

Butter Nut Snowballs

It seems every culture has their own version of these, from Mexican Wedding Cookies to Russian Tea Cakes. In New England, these tender, buttery cookies are popular around the holidays because the powdered sugar gives them a festive, snowy appearance. If you don't have time to refrigerate the dough, you can skip it, but you'll end up with something more akin to a snow globe than a snowball. They are equally delicious.

MAKES ABOUT 3 DOZEN

- 1 cup chopped unsalted walnuts (or pecans, almonds, shagbark hickory nuts, butternuts, or black walnuts)
- 2 sticks (1 cup) unsalted butter, at cool room temperature
- ½ cup confectioner's sugar, sifted, plus 1 cup for dusting
- 1 teaspoon vanilla extract
- ½ teaspoon fine sea salt
- 2 cups all-purpose flour, sifted

Preheat the oven to 350°F. Grease or line two baking sheets with parchment paper.

Finely grind the nuts in a food processor (or chop as finely as you can by hand).

With an electric mixer (preferably fitted with a paddle attachment), cream the butter and confectioner's sugar in a large bowl, starting on low and then increasing to medium speed, until fluffy, 1–2 minutes. Beat in the vanilla and salt. Add the ground nuts and mix on medium until combined. Add the flour and mix on low just until the dough starts to come together. (If the dough is too crumbly to hold together when gently pressed, mix in up to 1 tablespoon milk.) Chill the dough in the refrigerator for 30 minutes so the cookies hold their round shape better.

Using a tablespoon or ½-ounce cookie scoop, portion the dough and roll it into 1-inch balls with your hands. Arrange on the prepared pans at least 1 inch apart. Bake until the bottoms just start to color and the tops look dry, but before they start to crack too much, 10–14 minutes. Let them cool 10–15 minutes on the pan.

Sift the remaining 1 cup of confectioner's sugar into a shallow bowl. While still warm, roll the cookies in the sugar, turning to coat thickly and evenly. The sugar will appear to melt right onto the surface. Once the cookies have fully cooled, they can be rolled in confectioner's sugar a second time for a more powdery finish, if desired. Cool completely. Store in airtight containers at room temperature for 4–5 days.

Chocolate Fudge

I've been making fudge since I was in high school. It was one of the first and only things I learned how to make, even if it was a cheater's version made with marshmallows. This recipe is for real, old-fashioned chocolate fudge that firms up into creamy blocks. There are no marshmallows or corn syrup in sight, which means it takes a little practice to achieve that perfect, fudgy texture. I recommend using a candy thermometer to maximize your chances of success (test it first for accuracy by submerging the probe in boiling water to make sure it registers 212°F). Novice candymakers may want to start by trying a half-batch in a loaf pan to get the hang of it (temperatures will be the same, but the cooking and cooling times will be cut in half). Or you can find my foolproof marshmallow-based recipe on my blog (foodonthefood.com).

MAKES ABOUT 3 POUNDS

4 cups granulated sugar

2 cups heavy cream

12 ounces bittersweet or semisweet chopped chocolate or chocolate chips

1 stick (½ cup) unsalted butter, cut into 8 pieces

½ teaspoon salt

2 teaspoons vanilla extract

Line an 8 × 8-inch square pan with aluminum foil. Set a small bowl half-full of water and a pastry brush by the stove.

In a medium heavy-bottomed saucepan (at least 4-quart), combine the sugar, cream, chocolate, butter, and salt. Stir with a wooden spoon over medium-low heat until the sugar dissolves and bubbles start to form around the edges. This should take 12–18 minutes (it's okay if it takes longer, but if it takes much less, reduce the heat).

Once it comes to a simmer, stop stirring, and insert a candy thermometer. Use a wet pastry brush to wash down the sides of the pan to remove all the sugar residue splashed on the sides (this prevents the sugar from recrystallizing later). Continue to simmer over medium-low heat without stirring until the temperature reaches 234°F. This should take 6–12 minutes. (You can also test it by spooning a bit of the hot mixture into cold water. Let the mixture cool a few seconds and it should form a soft, squishable ball.) Immediately remove the pot from the heat.

Add the vanilla to the pot, but do not stir it in. Let it cool undisturbed for 1½–2 hours until the temperature goes down to 125°F–130°F.

The History of Fudge

Fudge-like confections have been around since the advent of sugar (see Penuche on page 177). But the smooth, creamy chocolate fudge sold all over New England was popularized in the late 19th century by students attending elite women's colleges in the Northeast. The Seven Sisters, as they were called, were created to provide women with the same educational opportunities as the Ivy League colleges that were, at that time, traditionally male. Emelyn Hartridge of Vassar College in New York is credited with starting the fudge-making frenzy in 1888, which soon spread to Massachusetts colleges, including Radcliffe, Wellesley, Mount Holyoke, and Smith. Wellesley College founder Henry Durant once declared that "pies, lies, and doughnuts should never have a place in Wellesley College." Undeterred, Wellesley women stayed up past curfew in their dorms cooking fudge in secret over alcohol burners and gas lamps. These accomplished young ladies brought their appetites for fudge back to their home states and beyond. The rest, as they say, is history.

Using a clean (this is important) and sturdy wooden spoon, stir the mixture until the vanilla is incorporated. Continue stirring for 5–15 minutes more as the mixture starts to thicken enough that the spoon creates a track when you stir and a spoonful drizzled back into the pot holds its shape for a few seconds before sinking back into the mixture. Before it loses its gloss, pour the mixture into the prepared pan with a rubber spatula. Let it cool at room temperature then refrigerate until cold and set.

To serve, lift up the foil to remove the fudge from the pan, then peel off the foil. Cut the fudge into square blocks on a cutting board with a sharp knife (run the knife under hot water and wipe it off between slices for clean cuts). Keep the fudge refrigerated until ready to serve. Store the fudge in an airtight container in the refrigerator for up to 1 week.

Mulled Pears

Pears steeped in mulled wine make a tasty seasonal topping for ice cream, or a winter-themed shortcake using the recipe on page 26. Because pears cook so quickly, these benefit from an overnight "cold brew" in the refrigerator to really absorb the warm spicing and achieve a deep mauve color. Make the day beforehand if possible. The cooking liquid is reduced to a syrup to concentrate the flavors of red wine, cinnamon, cloves, ginger, and orange, but you can flavor any way you like, swapping in lemon peel, allspice berries, and star anise. Any pears will do, but I recommend Boscs because they hold together best and have an elegant shape. To check for ripeness, gently squeeze the neck of the pear near the stem to see if it gives.

SERVES 4–6

1 cup red wine

1 cup water

1 cup granulated sugar

2 tablespoons brandy

2 cinnamon sticks

4 whole cloves

1-inch piece of fresh ginger, peeled, split in half

2½-inch-wide strips of orange peel (shave off the bitter white pith with a paring knife)

3 ripe Bosc pears, peeled, halved lengthwise along the core

Select a medium saucepan big enough to fit the 6 pear halves lying down the long way (but don't add them yet). Combine the wine, water, sugar, brandy, cinnamon, cloves, ginger, and orange peel. Stir over medium heat until the sugar dissolves. Bring to a simmer, then reduce the heat to low. Cook 10–15 minutes uncovered until slightly reduced and fragrant.

Meanwhile, with a melon baller or small spoon, scoop the seeds out of the pear halves. Using tongs, gently set the pears flat-side-down in the cooking liquid. The liquid should cover the pears about halfway (if not, add wine and water in equal amounts until it does). Bring the cooking liquid back up to a simmer and cook about 10–12 minutes more, uncovered, flipping the pears once after the first 5 minutes, until tender when pierced with a fork. Remove the pears and set in a shallow bowl. Let cool. Cut into wedges if desired.

Increase the heat to medium and continue to simmer the cooking liquid with the whole spices until it reduces to about 1¼ cups and looks syrupy, about 10 minutes. Let cool. Remove the whole spices and pour about ⅓ of the liquid over the pears. Store the remaining liquid in a separate jar so it doesn't get diluted by the pear's juices. Cover and refrigerate both overnight.

Serve the pears over vanilla or buttermilk ice cream, or the shortcake (page 26) in lieu of strawberries. Top with additional syrup from the jar. Any remaining syrup can be used in cocktails or served over pancakes or Greek yogurt.

Rosemary Juniper Shortbread

I developed these cookies to remind me of the shady New Hampshire backyard of my early childhood. I chose rosemary for its evergreen color and piney flavor, dried juniper berries for their bright, resiny pops of bitterness that cut the richness of the butter. Common juniper is an evergreen conifer shrub that ranges throughout New England. The berries (technically tiny, fleshy cones) are what give gin its herbal flavor. These would make a lovely addition to a holiday cookie plate. Don't let the butter sit out too long at room temperature (1 hour is sufficient) to prevent the dough from getting too crumbly.

**MAKES ABOUT 2 DOZEN
(RECIPE CAN BE DOUBLED)**

1 teaspoon juniper berries

1 tablespoon coarsely chopped fresh rosemary

1 stick (½ cup) unsalted butter, at cool room temperature

⅓ cup granulated sugar

1 cup all-purpose flour

¼ teaspoon fine sea salt

Coarse sea salt for sprinkling

Crush the juniper berries a few at a time with the back of a chef's knife (lay the flat side of the knife, with the blade facing away, directly on top of the berries, and give it a whack with the side of your fist). Finely chop the crushed berries. Mix with the chopped rosemary in a small bowl.

Cream the butter and sugar with an electric mixer (preferably fitted with a paddle attachment) on medium until smooth, 1–2 minutes. Add the rosemary and juniper berries, and blend on low until dispersed. Fluff up the flour with a whisk before measuring, then mix in the flour and salt on low just until the dough holds together. On a sheet of parchment or waxed paper, gather the dough into a log about 2 inches in diameter. (If your dough is too crumbly, you can mix in a bit of water or milk.) Roll up the dough in the paper, twist the ends to close, and chill in the refrigerator at least 1 hour.

Preheat the oven to 350°F. Grease or line a cookie sheet with parchment paper. With a sharp knife, slice the log into ¼- to ½-inch-thick rounds. Arrange them on the prepared pan about 1 inch apart. Sprinkle with flaky sea salt.

Bake 15–20 minutes until golden on the bottom and dry and firm on top when gently pressed. Remove from the oven and let cool. Cookies can be stored in an airtight container at room temperature for 1–2 weeks.

Banana Walnut Cupcakes with Penuche Frosting

Banana bread is a New England staple, despite the fact that bananas don't grow anywhere near our northern climes. Like banana bread, these cupcakes are a convenient and delicious use for overripe bananas, which every New Englander seems to have. Don't have time to make them? Throw those bananas in the freezer until you do (the skins will turn black, but the fruit is fine to use). I've gussied up these cupcakes with penuche frosting and chopped walnuts, but you could easily skip the frosting and call them muffins, or bake the batter in a standard loaf pan for an hour and call it bread. For best results, don't make the frosting until the cupcakes are fully cooled and ready to frost.

MAKES 8–10 STANDARD-SIZED CUPCAKES

For the cupcakes:

3 medium overripe bananas

¾ cup granulated sugar

1 stick (½ cup) unsalted butter, melted

1 large egg, at room temperature

1 teaspoon vanilla extract

1⅓ cups all-purpose flour

½ teaspoon baking powder

½ teaspoon baking soda

½ teaspoon salt

¼ teaspoon ground cinnamon

⅔ cup chopped walnuts

For the frosting:

4 tablespoons unsalted butter

½ cup light brown sugar, firmly packed

2 tablespoons milk

¼ teaspoon vanilla extract

Preheat the oven to 350°F. Line a standard muffin pan with liners.

If the bananas are frozen, defrost them in the microwave in their skins so they lose their chill before unpeeling. Whip the bananas in a large bowl with an electric mixer on medium-high for 1 minute. Add the sugar and whip for 2 minutes. Mix in the melted butter. Add the egg and vanilla, and mix well, scraping down the bottom and sides of the bowl before and after. Add the flour, baking powder, baking soda, salt, and cinnamon. Mix on low just until combined. Stir in the nuts by hand.

Fill the muffin wells ¾ of the way up (a 1½-ounce cookie scoop works well for this). Bake 20–25 minutes, until the tops are golden-brown and a toothpick inserted into the center comes out with no raw batter, only moist crumbs. Let cool completely.

For the frosting, melt the butter in a small saucepan over medium-low heat. Stir in the brown sugar with a wooden spoon. Bring to a boil, stirring frequently, and cook 1–2 minutes until foamy. Stir in the milk and bring to a boil. Cook 1 minute more, stirring constantly and scraping any hardened sugar from the bottom of the pan. Remove the pan from the heat and let cool 20–30 minutes (it should still be warm).

Pinch of table salt

¾–1 cup confectioner's sugar, sifted

Finely chopped walnuts for sprinkling (optional)

With an electric mixer, beat in the vanilla, salt, and confectioner's sugar, a little at a time. (If the frosting gets too thick or clumps up, add a splash of milk and continue mixing.) Spread the frosting on the cupcakes immediately and sprinkle with chopped walnuts if desired. Serve immediately or store covered at room temperature for 4–5 days.

Tapioca Pudding

This classic pudding was my grandfather's favorite dessert, but the consistency created by the chewy tapioca beads isn't for everyone. If you like rice pudding, you'll find it similar in flavor and texture. In addition to my interpretation of the classic New England milk pudding, I've also included a Thai milk tea variation for bubble tea lovers. You can usually find small tapioca pearls in the baking section of the grocery store, but I've also found them in the ethnic section near the rice and noodles. You want the little spherical beads, not the flour, to get the traditional texture. There seems to be variability in cooking times depending on the brand. I tested this recipe using Bob's Red Mill tapioca, which is fairly widely distributed, as well as Asian Best Brand. If you use something different, I recommend following the package's instructions for soaking and cooking times, as well as the ratio of tapioca to milk. If no instructions are listed, I suggest an overnight soak, then cook until the tapioca pearls are translucent and pleasantly chewy and the base thickens to a loose pudding consistency (it will thicken even more as it cools). To make this naturally gluten-free pudding dairy-free, you can substitute coconut milk.

SERVES 4–6

⅓ cup small pearl tapioca (not instant or Minute tapioca)
2 egg yolks
3½ cups milk (not skim)
½ cup granulated sugar
Pinch of salt
1 teaspoon vanilla extract
Pinch of cinnamon

Soak the tapioca at least 2 hours (up to overnight) in 2 cups of cold water. Drain.

In a medium, heavy-bottomed saucepan, thoroughly whisk the egg yolks with ¼ cup of the milk off heat. Whisk in the rest of the milk, sugar, and salt. Add the soaked tapioca.

Slowly bring the mixture to a simmer over medium-low heat, stirring constantly with a wooden spoon. This should take 10–15 minutes. Adjust the heat to maintain a bare simmer, and cook about 1 minute more for a looser pudding and 3 minutes for a thicker one, stirring frequently to prevent scorching, until the pudding has thickened and the tapioca is translucent and pleasantly chewy.

Remove the pan from the heat, and stir in the vanilla and cinnamon. Let cool (it will thicken further). Serve warm, room temperature, or cold. Store covered in the refrigerator 3–4 days.

The New England Connection: Tapioca

Tapioca is made from the starch of the cassava (yucca) plant, which is native to Brazil. It's also grown in many other tropical regions around the world, including Asia (the boba in bubble tea is tapioca-based). While tapioca isn't a New England ingredient in the agricultural sense, it's been available through trade for hundreds of years. Its use in pudding was carried over from the British—one of the earliest mentions of tapioca pudding is found in the 1861 British cookbook, *Mrs. Beeton's Book of Household Management*. Associated with bland flavor and easy digestion, tapioca has maintained a good reputation among the old, very young, and infirm. In fact, when faced with an ailing sailor as a boarder in the late 1800s, Boston resident Susan Stavers took a coffee grinder to some cassava roots, pulverizing them into fine, quick-cooking grounds that required no soaking and made a smoother pudding. The result was met with great fanfare, and she sold her tapioca grounds in paper bags door to door. In 1894, Stavers sold the rights to her tapioca discovery to John Whitman, a local publisher and grocer, who patented the method and created the Minute Tapioca Company in Orange, Massachusetts. The factory was closed in 1967, but the product is still produced today by Kraft Heinz.

Variation

Thai Milk Tea: Before soaking the tapioca, bring the milk to a bare simmer in a small pot. Remove from the heat and add 3 tea bags of black tea, 1 star anise, and 5 green cardamom pods, lightly crushed with the back of a knife or mortar and pestle (or ¼ teaspoon ground cardamom). Let steep for 5 minutes. Remove the tea bags. Pour the milk through a strainer into a bowl. Whisk the tapioca, sugar, and salt into the warm milk, and let soak 1 hour at room temperature to overnight in the refrigerator. In a medium, heavy-bottomed saucepan, whisk the egg yolks with ¼ cup of the tapioca mixture. Then whisk in the rest of the tapioca mixture. Proceed with the cooking process.

Cranberry Walnut Steamed Pudding with Maple Sauce

~~~~~~

Steamed pudding is basically a cake that you cook on the stovetop with moist heat instead of the oven's dry heat. Steaming was common back in the days when ovens weren't standard issue in the home kitchen, but the technique still comes in handy during the holidays when your oven is otherwise occupied. This pudding is bedecked with tart cranberries, crunchy walnuts, and fragrant cinnamon and orange zest. Perhaps my favorite part of the steamed pudding experience is the sauce—this one's heavy on the maple—which may be drizzled lightly or, if you're like me, liberally (my friend Shona adds a tablespoon or two of whiskey to cut the sweetness). You can find old (and barely used) pudding molds at thrift shops and antiques stores throughout New England. They look like fancy cake pans and come in tin, copper, and ceramic. Just remember to grease them well so the pudding releases easily, and then soak the pan immediately after unmolding so cleanup isn't a headache. This pudding recipe may be doubled for a 6-cup pudding mold, just increase the cooking time to 1½–2 hours.

SERVES 6-8

For the pudding:
1 cup all-purpose flour

½ cup plain bread crumbs

2 teaspoons baking powder

1 teaspoon orange zest

½ teaspoon table salt

½ teaspoon ground cinnamon

Pinch of ground cloves

1 stick (½ cup) unsalted butter, at cool room temperature

½ cup light brown sugar, firmly packed

1 large egg, at room temperature

⅓ cup milk, at room temperature

Set a large stockpot or Dutch oven by the sink with a rack in the bottom (or enough canning rings to support a pudding mold off the bottom of the pot). The pot must have a lid. Grease or spray a 3½-cup pudding mold or heatproof bowl with oil.

In a medium bowl, whisk together the flour, bread crumbs, baking powder, orange zest, salt, cinnamon, and cloves.

With an electric mixer (preferably fitted with a paddle attachment), cream the butter on medium-high for 1 minute. Add the brown sugar and continue creaming for 2 minutes. Scraping down the bottom and sides of the bowl as necessary, add the egg and beat 4–5 minutes until fluffy and light-colored. Add half of the dry ingredients and mix on low speed. With the mixer running on low, gradually add the milk down the side of the bowl. Add the rest of the dry ingredients and mix on low until incorporated. Fold in the cranberries and walnuts with a spatula.

Scrape the batter into the prepared pudding mold, cover loosely with foil, and secure foil with string. Set the pudding

1 cup fresh or frozen
cranberries (defrosted)

⅓ cup chopped walnuts

For the sauce:

1 stick (½) cup unsalted
butter

⅓ cup dark maple syrup

2 tablespoons light brown
sugar, firmly packed

¾ cup heavy cream

¼ teaspoon kosher salt

mold on the rack in the pot. Fill the pot with 2 inches of hot water (it's okay if the water touches the pudding tin, but it doesn't have to). Carefully set on the stove. Cover the pot with the lid, bring the water to a simmer over high heat, then reduce the heat to medium-low to keep the water bubbling.

Steam for about 1 hour or until a toothpick comes out clean. (To check, carefully remove the pudding mold from the pot using oven mitts—be careful of the hot steam!—and remove the string and foil.) Once done, remove the mold from the pot and let the pudding sit in the mold for 15 minutes.

To unmold, set a serving plate over the mold (again, using oven mitts), and, while holding the two firmly together, flip. If the pudding doesn't release right away, give it 5 minutes for gravity to assist.

For the sauce, melt the butter in a small saucepan over medium heat. Whisk in the maple syrup, brown sugar, heavy cream, and salt. Heat just to a gentle simmer (small bubbles around the edges), then reduce the heat to low and cook no more than 1 minute until thickened slightly. Remove from the heat.

Slice and serve the pudding, with or without whipped cream or vanilla ice cream, with some sauce drizzled over the top and additional sauce passed at the table. The pudding can be stored, covered, at room temperature 2–3 days. Microwave gently to rewarm. The sauce should be kept refrigerated and reheated gently on the stove or in the microwave, whisking until homogenous.

Peppermint Stick Ice Cream

This festive, frosty flavor is a childhood favorite. Its cool, minty taste brings to mind the excitement and joy of the holiday season and proves that ice cream isn't just for the summertime. If candy canes are out of season, look for starlight mints, red-and-white round candies that pack the same pepperminty punch, or buy them online. Just make sure your candy canes aren't the fruit-flavored ones! For best results, start the day before you want to serve it to allow enough time to make the base, churn it, and freeze. For tips on making homemade ice cream, see page 189.

MAKES ABOUT 1 QUART

- 2 cups heavy cream, divided
- 2 large egg yolks
- 1 cup milk (preferably whole, but not skim)
- ¾ cup granulated sugar
- 1½ teaspoons peppermint extract
- ½ teaspoon vanilla extract
- 5 peppermint candy canes or ½ cup starlight mints, crushed finely

Add 1 cup of cream to a large bowl. Set a strainer over the bowl and place near the stove.

In a medium saucepan off heat, whisk the yolks, then slowly whisk in the milk. Whisk in the sugar. Stir in the remaining 1 cup of cream. Cook over medium heat, stirring constantly with a wooden spoon, until it comes to a bare simmer, 5–8 minutes.

Remove the pan from the heat. Pour the hot mixture into the nested sieve. Remove the sieve and stir in the peppermint and vanilla extracts. Chill, covered, in the refrigerator until cold, 4–6 hours or overnight.

Freeze in an ice cream maker according to the manufacturer's instructions. While the ice cream is churning, put the peppermint candies into a resealable plastic bag and zip it tight. Smash them with a meat mallet or a can into pieces ¼ inch or smaller. Stir in the candy pieces after the churning is complete.

Spoon into a freezer-safe container and freeze until firm, 4–6 hours. Store in the freezer for up to 1 month.

Note: For instructions on how to make ice cream without a machine, see page 190.

Variation

Easy No-Cook Version: Replace the egg yolks with 2 whole eggs (preferably pasteurized, since they will be raw). Whisk the eggs in a large bowl for 1–2 minutes until very frothy. Whisk in the sugar. Continue to whisk 1–2 minutes more until light-colored and thickened. Whisk in the milk, peppermint extract, and vanilla. Stir in the cream. Proceed to churning. (You can also leave the eggs out entirely and just mix everything together before churning.)

Butterscotch Blondies

Brown butter, dark brown sugar, and a heavy hand with the vanilla and salt make these blondies extra butterscotchy even before the addition of butterscotch chips. Contrary to popular belief, butterscotch did not traditionally contain Scotch, but adults are welcome to add a splash of whiskey. Perfect for after-school snacks or after-dinner ice cream sundaes, you'll want to keep this recipe on repeat all year long.

MAKES 16

1 stick (½ cup) unsalted butter, cut into pieces

¾ cup dark brown sugar, firmly packed

1 large egg

1 tablespoon vanilla extract

1 cup all-purpose flour

½ teaspoon baking soda

½ teaspoon kosher salt

½ cup butterscotch chips

½ cup bittersweet chocolate chips

½ cup chopped walnuts

Flaky sea salt, for sprinkling

Preheat the oven to 350°F. Grease an 8 × 8-inch pan or line with parchment if desired.

In a small heavy-bottomed saucepan (preferably without a dark nonstick coating), melt the butter over medium-low heat. Continue cooking 5–10 minutes, stirring occasionally in the beginning and more frequently later on, scraping the bottom and sides of the pot with a wooden spoon, until the butter browns and smells toasty. Once the butter foams, the solids on the bottom will start to brown quickly—watch closely so they don't burn. If you have a hard time seeing the color of the butter, spoon some out onto a white plate, being sure to scrape some of the solids from the bottom of the pan. Remove from the heat and pour the butter into a large mixing bowl.

With a wooden spoon, immediately stir the brown sugar into the melted butter while hot. Let cool slightly, then whisk in the egg and vanilla until well blended.

Add the flour, baking soda, and salt. Stir in about halfway, then add the butterscotch chips, chocolate chips, and nuts. Stir until the chips and nuts are well dispersed and the dry ingredients are fully mixed in. Spread the batter evenly in the prepared pan. Sprinkle with flaky sea salt if desired.

Bake 22–28 minutes until a toothpick inserted into the center comes out clean or with only moist crumbs attached (no raw batter). Let cool. Blondies can be stored in an airtight container at room temperature 4–5 days.

Penuche

This gloriously smooth and creamy brown sugar fudge is a New England favorite and predates the popular chocolate version. It's incredibly sweet—a little goes a long way—but the browning reactions that occur during the cooking process create a complex, caramelized flavor I find very enticing. A candy thermometer will dramatically increase your chances of success (test it first for accuracy by submerging the probe in boiling water to make sure it registers 212°F), but I've included tips for how to make it without one. Feel free to add chopped nuts during the stirring process. Walnuts or pecans would be delicious, as would hickory nuts, butternuts, or even black walnuts. For clean cuts, run a sharp knife (the thinner, the better) under hot water and wipe off the blade between each cut. Note that this recipe makes about half as much as the chocolate fudge recipe because it doesn't keep quite as long and it's much sweeter.

MAKES 1½ POUNDS

2 cups light brown sugar, firmly packed

1 cup granulated sugar

1 cup heavy cream

4 tablespoons unsalted butter, cut into 4 pieces

¼ teaspoon table salt

1 teaspoon vanilla extract

Line a standard 9½ × 5½-inch loaf pan with parchment paper all the way up the sides. Set a small bowl half-full of water and a pastry brush by the stove.

In a medium heavy-bottomed saucepan, combine the sugars, cream, butter, and salt over medium-low heat. Stir constantly until the sugar dissolves and bubbles form, about 5–10 minutes.

Once it comes to a simmer, stop stirring and insert a candy thermometer. Wash the sugary residue from the sides of the pan with a wet brush (you don't want any sugar crystals present or they can trigger recrystallization later). Simmer without stirring, about 5–10 minutes until the mercury reaches 236°F, or until the mixture holds together in a soft, squishy ball when a spoonful is dropped into cold water (let it cool a few seconds in the water before touching). Immediately remove the pan from the heat.

Without stirring it in, add the vanilla. Let cool for about 1 hour or until the pot is still warm but not too hot to hold your hand against it (110°F–115°F).

With a clean (this is important) and sturdy wooden spoon, beat 5–10 minutes until the mixture thickens and lightens in color (it will go from looking like caramel sauce to something more like creamy peanut butter). Before the mixture gets too

The New England Connection: Penuche

Penuche is thought to have its roots with the Portuguese immigrants that arrived in New England from the Azores starting in the 1800s. They settled largely in New Bedford and Fall River, Massachusetts, as well as coastal Rhode Island and Connecticut, first for the whaling industry and, later, in much larger numbers, to work in the textile mills of Lawrence and Lowell during the Industrial Revolution. Indeed, penuche bears a striking resemblance to traditional Azorean *caramelos*, a fudge-like confection made by cooking sugar with milk and butter until it caramelizes, sets, and can be cut into little squares. Penuche is also well known on the Hawaiian islands, where Portuguese immigrants from the Azores and Madeira islands were recruited to work in the sugarcane fields. Where the name comes from, however, is unclear. The word "penuche" is similar to the Spanish word for brown sugar, which is what we traditionally use in New England to make this fudge, presumably because it was cheaper (and more flavorful) than white sugar.

stiff and loses all of its gloss, pour it into the lined pan and let cool. Refrigerate until the fudge sets.

To serve, lift up the parchment to remove the fudge from the pan. Cut the fudge on a cutting board into small square blocks with a sharp knife (run the knife under hot water and wipe it off for cleaner cuts). Keep the fudge refrigerated until ready to serve. Store in an airtight container in the refrigerator for 3–4 days.

Cranberry Pine Nut Biscotti

Dried cranberries are a favorite local alternative to raisins, and it's not unusual to see them pop up in holiday cookie plates due to their festive color and tart flavor. Here I've added them to traditional Italian biscotti, a cookie that's become almost as common as chocolate chip thanks to the substantial Italian-American presence in New England. Biscotti means "twice cooked," meaning it is first baked as a log, then sliced and baked again, giving it its crisp texture. Pine nuts, found in the cones of the pinyon pine and stone pine, are a traditional Italian ingredient, but they also draw a nice parallel to the piney forests of New England. Our local pines also produce nuts, but they're generally too small to be worth collecting. If you don't have pine nuts, you can substitute almonds or pistachios. A drizzle of white chocolate makes them extra fancy, but it's optional.

MAKES ABOUT 2 DOZEN

- 1¾ cups all-purpose flour
- 1 teaspoon baking powder
- ¼ teaspoon table salt
- ⅛ teaspoon ground cinnamon
- 4 tablespoons unsalted butter, at cool room temperature
- ¾ cup granulated sugar
- 2 large eggs
- 2 teaspoons vanilla extract
- ½ teaspoon almond extract
- ¾ cup dried cranberries
- ⅓ cup pine nuts
- ¾ cup white chocolate chips, for drizzling (optional)

Preheat the oven to 325°F. Grease or line a cookie sheet with parchment paper.

In a small bowl, whisk together the flour, baking powder, salt, and cinnamon.

With an electric mixer (preferably fitted with a paddle attachment), cream the butter and sugar on medium speed for 1–2 minutes. Scraping down the bottom and sides of the bowl as needed, mix in the eggs and extracts. Continue mixing for 1 minute on medium speed. Add the cranberries and pine nuts and mix on low speed until evenly dispersed. Add the dry ingredients to the butter mixture and mix on low just until combined.

Turn the dough out onto a well-floured surface. Gather the dough together with floured hands, cut it in half, and form it into two slightly flattened logs about 12 inches long, 2 inches wide, and 1 inch high. Try to keep the ends the same width as the middle rather than tapering off so the finished cookies are a uniform size. Set the logs on the prepared pan about 3 inches apart.

Bake for 20–25 minutes until lightly golden, firm, and just starting to crack. Remove from the oven and let cool 10 minutes.

One at a time, transfer the logs to a cutting board (you might need two spatulas). Cut each with a serrated knife at an angle into slices ¾ inch thick. Return the slices to the baking sheet on their sides. Bake 10–15 minutes longer until lightly golden. Let cool completely.

For the white chocolate drizzle, melt the white chocolate chips in the microwave in short 30-second bursts at 50% power, stirring in between until melted. Drizzle the white chocolate over the biscotti with a whisk or fork, or scoop into a resealable bag, seal, and snip off the tip of the corner to create a mini-piping bag. Let the chocolate dry completely. Store in airtight containers at room temperature for 1–2 weeks.

Needhams (Maine Potato Candy)

While candy made from potatoes might not seem especially appetizing, I can assure you, after winning over my very skeptical husband and one very snarky teenaged son, these are amazing. They're basically Mounds bars, but better. Here, one potato (mashed) serves to bind together the sweetened, shredded coconut filling before it's enrobed in chocolate. You won't even notice the potato is there, I promise. Tempering chocolate (the temperature-based process of stabilizing chocolate for candy-making) can be a bit fussy. For easy dipping without having to temper chocolate, I recommend using special melting chocolate disks, but you can use regular untempered chocolate if you melt it very gently in the microwave. If it overheats, the coating won't be as shiny and crisp, and it may develop gray bloomy streaks. (It's perfectly fine to eat; it just doesn't look as fancy.)

MAKES ABOUT 18 LARGE OR 36 SMALL CANDIES

1 medium-sized russet potato (at least ½ pound)

2 cups confectioner's sugar, sifted

2 cups shredded, sweetened coconut, firmly packed

1 teaspoon vanilla extract

¼ teaspoon fine sea salt

Dark chocolate melting wafers

For large candies (1½-inch square), line a standard loaf pan with parchment paper that hangs over the sides so it can be pulled out easily. For smaller candies (¾-inch square), do the same with an 8 × 8-inch pan. (Full disclosure: Smaller candies take twice as long to coat in chocolate—but you do end up with twice as many!)

In a pot of boiling water, cook the potato whole until tender all the way through when pierced with a fork (this can take 30–40 minutes depending on the size and shape of your potato). Let cool until still warm but easily handled. Peel the potato, then put it through a ricer or food mill until smooth. (You can also push it through a standard-mesh sieve with a sturdy wooden spoon. Do not use a food processor or blender—the potato will turn out gluey.)

Measure out ⅓ cup of mashed potato. If cold, reheat the potato in the microwave, just until warm. Stir in the confectioner's sugar, coconut, vanilla, and salt with a wooden spoon until well mixed. The mixture should be moist. If not, keep mixing until no longer dry. Press the mixture into the prepared pans and freeze for 20–30 minutes. Remove the pan from the freezer and cut with a sharp knife into pieces. Freeze again for 20–30 minutes.

The History of Needhams

These potato candies were originally invented in Auburn, Maine, in the 1870s when a cook who worked for confectioner John Seavey at Seavey's Sweets came up with a recipe for coconut creams—with a spud-based twist. The potato has long been one of Maine's top agricultural products, and this confection was one of many industrious ways to use the versatile tuber. The candies, which are always cut into squares, became an instant hit. Seavey reportedly named the candies after a popular preacher of the time, George C. Needham, but I can't help but think the name stuck due to its obvious marketing appeal, since the name explicitly states that you "need 'em." Which, for the record, you do.

Meanwhile, melt the chocolate in a bowl in the microwave in 30-second increments at 50% power, stirring in between until melted. (If you stop heating when the chips are mostly—but not entirely—melted, you can keep stirring to melt the rest of the chocolate without losing the temper.) Alternatively, you can melt your chocolate in a metal bowl set over a small saucepan with an inch of gently simmering water. The bottom of the bowl should not touch the water.

Remove the coconut mixture from the freezer. Remove the parchment from the pan and separate the candies with a knife. One at a time, dip the candies in melted chocolate, remove with a fork, and set on parchment or waxed paper to dry. If the chocolate starts to harden in the bowl before you're done, you can gently reheat in the microwave. Try to pull out any pieces of coconut that fall into the chocolate as you go so the candy coating is smooth and appealing. Candies can be stored at room temperature for 2 days, 4–5 in the refrigerator.

Maple Walnut Fudge

This recipe is the real deal (real cream, real butter, real maple syrup). Be warned: It's very sweet—just a few steps away from pure maple sugar candy—but the flavor is swoonworthy. I recommend using a candy thermometer—it'll save you from wasting expensive ingredients, and they're very easy to use (test it first for accuracy by submerging the probe in boiling water to make sure it registers 212°F). Be sure to use a big enough saucepan, since the mixture quadruples in volume as it cooks, preferably more tall than wide so there's enough depth for your candy thermometer to get a good reading. If your pan is too small, the mixture will boil over and make a huge mess (I speak from experience). It requires a little attention and elbow grease, but this fudge is much better than what you'd buy at many tourist shops. (Shh, don't tell!)

MAKES 2¼ POUNDS

2½ cups granulated sugar

2 cups heavy cream

1 cup pure maple syrup (the darker, the better)

¼ teaspoon salt

4 tablespoons unsalted butter

1 teaspoon vanilla extract

½ cup chopped walnuts

Line an 8 × 8-inch baking pan with aluminum foil. Set a small bowl half-full of water and a pastry brush by the stove.

In a medium to large heavy-bottomed saucepan (at least 4 quarts), combine the sugar, cream, maple syrup, and salt. Stir with a wooden spoon over medium heat until the sugar dissolves and bubbles start to form around the edges. This should take 8–10 minutes (if it takes much less, reduce the heat).

Once it comes to a simmer, stop stirring and insert a candy thermometer. Wash the sugary residue from the sides of the pan with a wet pastry brush (you don't want any sugar crystals present or they can trigger recrystallization later). Continue to cook without stirring until the temperature reaches 237°F (soft ball stage). This should take 10–20 minutes. (You can also test it by spooning a bit of the hot mixture into cold water. Give it a few seconds to cool and it should form a soft ball you can squish between your fingers.) Immediately move the pot from the heat before it surpasses 240°F.

Add the butter and vanilla, but do not stir. Let cool undisturbed for 1–2 hours, until the pot is barely warm at all (100°F to 110°F seems to be the sweet spot).

Using a clean (this is important) and sturdy wooden spoon, stir the mixture until the butter and vanilla are incorporated.

Then stir in the nuts. Continue stirring for 3–10 minutes until the mixture starts to thicken, lighten in color, and lose some of its gloss. Before it turns completely matte, scrape the mixture into the prepared pan with a rubber spatula. Let cool at room temperature then refrigerate until cold and set.

To serve, lift up the foil to remove the fudge from the pan, then peel off the foil. Cut the fudge into small square blocks on a cutting board with a sharp knife (run it under hot water and wipe it off between slices). Keep refrigerated until ready to serve. Store fudge in an airtight container in the refrigerator for up to 1 week.

Ice Cream for All Seasons

*M*y obsession with ice cream started young. If you asked me at age 4 to draw a crude map of my New Hampshire town as I understood it in the 1970s, it would have featured my house dead center with the imprecise locations of every ice cream shop, musical truck, and novelty freezer in a 10-mile radius. I loved to gaze at the different flavors through the transparent cases at the local ice cream parlor. I was mesmerized by the deep swells of fluffy ice cream, charmed by their muted, pastel hues. Some were flecked with chocolate, nuts, or bits of fruit. Others oozed with thick swirls of butterscotch or fudge. It was like an edible artist's palette, seemingly bottomless and filled with sweet promise. I yearned to take a spoon, dip it into every pot, and paint the world with ice cream.

America's love for ice cream was born in New England as a regional obsession. The area's picturesque dairy farms produced some of the country's richest milk and cream. Our favorite ice cream flavors were inspired by the local bounty: strawberry, black raspberry, maple walnut. Ice, in high demand in the years before refrigeration, was harvested from frozen lakes and ponds in big blocks during the dead of winter. The ice was then stored in insulated icehouses year-round. Even the salt used to churn the ice cream was a New England product. Wind-powered saltworks popped up all over Cape Cod and other coastal areas of Massachusetts and Maine during Revolutionary times. No wonder New England continues to be one of the top ice cream–consuming regions in the country (and the world).

Making ice cream was a coveted summertime ritual made possible by communal effort around a hand-cranked churn. You'd pour the ice cream mixture into a metal canister, surround it with crushed ice and plenty of rock salt, and crank away. The salt lowered the melting point of the ice, creating an intense mini-freezer. The ice cream base would start freezing from the outside while the crank kept the mixture constantly moving to redistribute and break up any large ice crystals. Hand-cranking ice cream was no easy task, best accomplished as a team effort followed by a group reward.

This chapter celebrates ice cream as the all-season all-star it is. No longer do we limit our ice cream binges to the summertime—we indulge unapologetically all year round. We serve ice cream with pie, over brownies, and smushed between cookies. We blitz it into frappes. We make towering sundaes. We sprinkle it liberally with jimmies or chocolate shots. We love ice cream so much, it needed its own chapter.

While you'll find fleeting seasonal ice cream flavors scattered throughout the earlier chapters (like Rhubarb Ripple in "Spring" and Peach Amaretti in "Summer"), this chapter focuses on classic, kid-friendly ice cream flavors that can be mixed, matched, and made any time of year: Connecticut Valley Vanilla, Beantown Chocolate, New Hampshire Strawberry, Vermont Maple, Rhode Island Coffee, and Maine Buttermilk and Sea Salt. You'll also find traditional New England flavors like Mocha Chip, Pecan Penuche, Mint Chocolate Chip, and

Grape-Nuts. Don't forget the recipes for classic ice cream parlor toppings like hot fudge, salted caramel, and butterscotch sauce.

The Scoop on Making Ice Cream

Most of the ice cream recipes in this book feature a cooked custard base, which creates the richest-tasting ice cream. Before embarking on your own homemade ice cream adventure, keep in mind the following steps and their approximate time estimates to ensure your ice cream is completed by the time you want to serve it and has the proper consistency:

Prep: 1 hour to overnight. A few (but not all) recipes require fruit preparation, maceration, or overnight steeping to bring out the best flavor. Read through the recipe ahead of time to see if this applies.

Cook: 15 minutes to make the custard base.

Chill: 4–6 hours or overnight in the refrigerator (or 1 hour stirred over an ice bath). The mixture should be cold or it won't churn properly.

Churn: 30 minutes with an ice cream machine (or up to 3 hours without a machine). The mixture should be the consistency of applesauce.

Freeze: 6–8 hours in the freezer or overnight. It should be firm but scoopable.

For custard-style ice cream, I recommend starting 1–2 days before you plan to serve it so it's not too soft. But I've also included a number of quick, no-cook variations for the time-strapped ice cream lover. This farm-style method uses cold, raw ingredients, which eliminates the cooking and chilling process. If you start in the morning, you can have ice cream by dinner. It yields a less rich but very fresh-tasting ice cream. Just keep in mind that raw eggs can harbor pathogens like salmonella. Avoid serving ice cream with raw eggs to pregnant, elderly, or immunosuppressed individuals. Pasteurized eggs would be a good choice. Or you can leave out the eggs entirely and make Philadelphia-style ice cream.

My ice cream recipes call for heavy cream (also called heavy whipping cream) because it has a high butterfat content that yields a wonderful, creamy product. But I also call for some milk to keep the ice cream from getting *too* rich. I recommend whole milk (3% fat) or 2% for the best results, but I often end up using 1% since that's what I keep in the house, and that's fine, too. Feel free to use what you have on hand, but be warned that skim milk with 0% fat will yield an icier, thinner product more closely resembling ice milk.

Several of these recipes contain mix-ins, swirls, or other tasty layers. Mix-ins are generally added to the ice cream once churning is complete—just stir them in. Swirls and other layers are best added as you're packing the partially frozen ice cream into a container so they don't get overmixed. Simply alternate the base with the appropriate add-in layer as the recipe indicates. Don't be too neat. Variability looks more appealing. To swirl the layers, take a large spoon or knife and run it through the mixture in a single figure-eight motion, drawing the utensil first downward, then up towards the surface as you go. But even without swirling, you'll still get a ripple effect by simply scooping the layered ice cream out of the container.

Depending on your freezer settings, you may find it's best to let your ice cream sit out at room temperature for 5 minutes or so to thaw a bit before scooping. Be sure to return the container to the freezer immediately afterwards. Melted ice cream does not refreeze well.

For best results, I recommend buying an electric ice cream maker. As long as you follow the instructions, they consistently churn out finely textured, creamy ice cream with just the right amount of air mixed in to create that perfect, scoopable consistency we all know and love.

These days there are multiple models of hands-free ice cream machines to fit nearly every budget. I got my ice cream machine as a wedding gift 20 years ago, and my husband sometimes wonders aloud about which I love more, my ice cream machine or him. The design is simple: a rotating base, a canister insert that you freeze ahead of time, a dasher (part scraper, part mixer paddle), and a cover to keep everything in place. It works exactly the same way as an old-fashioned ice cream churn except you can go off and do something else while it spins away. The only caveat is you need to make sure the canister is frozen solid (2–4 days in the freezer is best—24 hours is not enough). I store mine in the freezer so it's always ready to go. Too many times I've had the ice cream cravings hit only to realize my freezer bowl is still in the dish rack or stored with the rest of the machine on a room-temperature shelf. Learn from my mistakes. More expensive models use a compressor to freeze the ice cream in their own self-contained refrigeration system.

When using an ice cream machine, be sure to follow the manufacturer's instructions. If the manual is long gone, you can tell when the ice cream in a canister-style machine is done when the motor labors loudly and the mixture starts to mound up in the middle of the bowl, pulling away from the sides. That's your cue to serve up delicious, pillowy soft-serve immediately or pack it away in the freezer to firm up for those quintessential ruffled scoops.

How to Make Ice Cream without a Machine

If an ice cream machine is simply not in the budget, or if space is an issue, you can still make great tasting ice cream at home. Here are three low-tech ways to get it done:

The Hands-Off Food Processor Method

Once you make your custard base, pour it into a resealable freezer bag, seal it up tight, and set it in a 9 × 13-inch metal roasting pan (or you can just pour it directly into the pan). Set it in the freezer on an even surface until it's completely frozen, 6–8 hours. Break the frozen custard into chunks and process them in a food processor until uniformly creamy. If there are some stubborn chunks, remove the rest of the ice cream to another container and continue processing the chunks until all the ice cream is smooth. For soft-serve, you can eat it right away. For firmer ice cream, transfer the mixture to a freezer-safe storage container and freeze 4–6 hours more. This method creates a smooth, dense, gelato-like texture.

The Bowl-in-the-Freezer Method

Pour the ice cream mixture into a large metal bowl, put it in the freezer, and whisk it well every half hour for 3–4 hours. Setting an alarm is helpful. Once it reaches the consistency of loose soft-serve, pour it into a long-term, freezer-safe, storage container and let it freeze undisturbed for 4–6 hours until firm. The texture of the final product depends on how often and how thoroughly you stir it during the freezing process. Lackadaisical or haphazard stirring yields a coarser product. To get a finer texture, stir more often.

DIY Ice Cream Churn

If you have a penchant for fun science projects, try this hybrid method, which combines the traditional, time-tested properties of ice and salt with the convenience of an electric mixer. Fill a large bowl halfway up with crushed ice (I use half of a 5-pound bag). Glass or plastic is best for the outer bowl (like the exterior base of a large salad spinner), but metal works, too. Add 1 cup of kosher salt to the ice. Mix until the ice starts to melt. Nestle a slightly smaller metal bowl down into the ice. Metal is key, preferably more deep than wide (I like to use the bowl of my stand mixer). There should be at least an inch of ice between the two bowls all the way around. Top off the gap between the two bowls with more ice as needed.

Add the ice cream mixture to the inner bowl. With an electric mixer, beat on low speed for 10 minutes. We're not trying to whip the cream, but rather lower the temperature of the mixture quickly. If it splatters, drape a dishtowel over everything while you mix. Set the entire two-bowl assembly in the freezer, ice and all. After 30 minutes, remove it from the freezer and mix again with the electric mixer, breaking up the icebergs, for 3–5 minutes. It should be the consistency of soft-serve. Make sure the beaters scrape the sides and bottom of the bowl as you go. Transfer to a freezer-safe container and freeze for 6–8 hours.

Root Beer Floa

Connecticut Valley Vanilla Ice Cream

The Connecticut River is the longest river in New England. It stretches from the Connecticut Lakes in the northern tip of New Hampshire, runs along the state's border with Vermont, down through Massachusetts and Connecticut, finally emptying in Long Island Sound. The surrounding Connecticut River Valley is known for its fertile soil and lush grass, perfect for grazing dairy cows and producing fresh milk and cream. Vanilla is the most popular ice cream flavor in New England due to its great taste and versatility. It's the ultimate accompaniment for pies, cobblers, and crisps. It's essential for Cornmeal Molasses Pudding (page 157). Plus, it makes a mean root beer float. For best results, start the day before you want to serve it to allow enough time to make the base, churn it, and freeze. For tips on making homemade ice cream, see page 189.

MAKES ABOUT 1 QUART

2 cups heavy cream, divided

2 large egg yolks

1 cup milk (preferably whole, but not skim)

¾ cup granulated sugar

Pinch of salt

2 teaspoons vanilla extract or vanilla bean paste

Add 1 cup of cream to a large bowl. Set a strainer over the bowl and place near the stove.

In a medium saucepan off heat, whisk the yolks, then slowly whisk in the milk. Gradually whisk in the sugar. Stir in the remaining 1 cup of cream and the salt. Cook over medium heat, stirring constantly with a wooden spoon, until it comes to a bare simmer, 8–12 minutes, and thickens enough to slightly coat the back of a spoon.

Pour the hot mixture into the strainer bowl. Remove the strainer and stir in the vanilla. Chill, covered, in the refrigerator until cold, 4–6 hours or overnight.

Freeze in an ice cream maker according to the manufacturer's instructions, then transfer to a freezer-safe container and freeze until firm, 6–8 hours. Store in the freezer for up to 1 month.

Note: For instructions on how to make ice cream without a machine, see page 190.

Variations

Easy No-Cook Vanilla: Replace the egg yolks with 2 whole eggs (preferably pasteurized, since they will be raw). In a large bowl, whisk the eggs for 1–2 minutes until frothy. Whisk in the sugar. Continue to whisk 1–2 minutes more until light-colored and thickened. Whisk in the milk, salt, and vanilla. Stir in the cream. Proceed to churning. (You can also leave the eggs out entirely and just mix everything together before churning.)

Chocolate Chip Cookie Dough: Inspired by the popular Ben & Jerry's flavor, start by beating 2 tablespoons of soft unsalted butter with ¼ cup light brown sugar with an electric mixer or a wooden spoon until fluffy, about 1 minute. Add 1 tablespoon heavy cream, ¼ teaspoon vanilla extract, and ⅛ teaspoon salt. Mix well. Add ¼ cup all-purpose flour and mix on low just until combined. Mix in 2 tablespoons (1 ounce) mini chocolate chips. Form the dough into ⅓-inch balls; you should have about 30. (You can make these a few days ahead of time and refrigerate or freeze them until ready to use.) When the ice cream is done churning, stir an additional 2 tablespoons mini chocolate chips into the ice cream. Add the cookie dough balls as you transfer the ice cream to a freezer-safe container, then freeze.

Cookies 'n' Cream: Add 1 cup crushed Oreo cookies during the last minute of churning, or stir them into the churned ice cream before freezing.

Chocolate-Covered Toffee: Add ½ cup (about 4 ounces) crushed chocolate-covered toffee bars (such as Heath or Skor) during the last minute of churning or stir them into the churned ice cream.

Moose Tracks: You can buy Moose Tracks ice cream at moosetracks.com, but here's a homemade version of the popular flavor: vanilla ice cream filled with peanut butter cups and fudge ripple. While the ice cream is churning, heat ¼ cup (2 ounces) of chopped bittersweet or semisweet chocolate or chocolate chips with ¼ cup heavy cream in the microwave in 30-second bursts, stirring after each burst. When fully melted and combined, set the chocolate ganache aside to cool. Meanwhile, chop 3 ounces peanut butter cups. Stir the chopped peanut butter cups into the churned ice cream and layer with the chocolate ganache while transferring to a freezer-safe container. Freeze until firm.

Root Beer Float: Add a scoop of vanilla ice cream to a tall glass and pour root beer over the top (go slow so you don't overflow the glass).

Beantown Chocolate Ice Cream

Boston is famous for its baked beans, but there was a time when the city was known for beans of another sort: cacao beans. The first chocolate factory in the country, Baker's Chocolate (originally, Hannon's Best Chocolates), was started in 1765 on the banks of the Neponset River. By the 1950s, Boston was the candy capital of America. There were at least 140 candy companies in the Boston area, according to the New England Historical Society, and many of them could be found along a stretch of Main Street in Cambridge known as "Confectioner's Row." Most of those companies are long gone, but the Bostonian passion for chocolate remains (see relative newcomer Taza Chocolate in nearby Somerville). This ice cream is deeply chocolatey, thanks to block chocolate and cocoa powder. Dutch-process cocoa has the best flavor and color for this ice cream recipe, but you can substitute regular unsweetened cocoa powder in a pinch. For best results, start the day before you want to serve it to allow enough time to make the base, churn it, and freeze. For tips on making homemade ice cream, see page 189.

MAKES ABOUT 1¼ QUARTS

4 ounces (about ⅔ cup) bittersweet or semisweet chocolate chips or chopped chocolate

2 cups heavy cream, divided

2 large egg yolks

1 cup milk (preferably whole, but not skim)

¾ cup granulated sugar

Pinch of salt

¼ cup Dutch-process cocoa powder

1 teaspoon vanilla extract

Melt the chocolate in a glass bowl in the microwave in 30-second increments, stirring in between, 1–2 minutes.

Add 1 cup of cream to a large bowl. Set a strainer over the bowl and place near the stove.

In a medium saucepan off heat, whisk the yolks, then slowly whisk in the milk. Whisk in the sugar. Stir in the remaining 1 cup of cream and the salt. Cook over medium heat, stirring constantly with a wooden spoon, until it comes to a bare simmer, 5–8 minutes.

Remove the pan from the heat and whisk in the cocoa powder until thoroughly combined. Then whisk in the melted chocolate, stirring until completely melted.

Pour the hot mixture into the strainer bowl. Remove the strainer and stir in the vanilla. Chill, covered, in the refrigerator until cold, 4–6 hours or overnight.

Freeze in an ice cream maker according to the manufacturer's instructions, then transfer to a freezer-safe container and freeze until firm, 6–8 hours. Store in the freezer for up to 1 month.

Note: For instructions on how to make ice cream without a machine, see page 190.

Variations

Easy No-Cook Chocolate: Melt the chocolate and 1 cup of the cream in the microwave in 30-second bursts until melted. Whisk until the chocolate fully dissolves. Set aside. Replace the egg yolks with 2 whole eggs (preferably pasteurized, since they will be raw). In a large bowl, whisk the eggs for 1–2 minutes until frothy. Whisk in the sugar. Continue to whisk 1–2 minutes more until light-colored and thickened. Add the cocoa powder to the milk and whisk well, then slowly whisk it into the egg mixture. Add the chocolate mixture, vanilla, and salt and whisk well. Stir in the cream. Proceed to churning. (For an egg-free alternative, just mix everything together and churn.)

Chocolate Malt: Substitute ⅓ cup malted milk powder (like Horlick's or Carnation) for the cocoa powder.

Chocolate Fudge Brownie: Inspired by the popular Ben & Jerry's flavor, start by making the Salted + Malted Chocolate Brownies (page 24) and let them cool. Then make the chocolate ice cream base. While the ice cream is churning, heat 2 ounces of chopped bittersweet or semisweet chocolate or chocolate chips with ¼ cup heavy cream in the microwave in 30-second bursts, stirring after each burst. When fully melted and combined, set the chocolate ganache aside to cool. Cut 2 or 3 brownies into small chunks. When transferring the churned ice cream to a container, layer it with the brownie chunks and ganache. Freeze.

Charles River Crunch: To create this cheeky flavor, Waltham, Massachusetts-based Lizzy's Ice Cream adds chunks of almond toffee to their dark chocolate ice cream. Chop 4 ounces Heath or Skor bars (about 3 bars), or Almond Roca. Add during the last minute of churning, or stir into the churned ice cream before freezing.

New Hampshire Strawberry Ice Cream

Though strawberries are grown all over New England, New Hampshire is where I tasted my first strawberry, homegrown in the backyard. From then on, I could be counted upon to strip the plants of their heart-shaped fruits before anybody else could get their hands on them. Strawberry season is short and fleeting, but ice cream is a great way to extend the season just a little bit longer. If the strawberry-picking window has already passed, there's no shame in using frozen strawberries. This version is strawberry-forward, as any good strawberry ice cream should be. I don't strain the seeds out because I like the texture they provide, but you can strain them out if you wish. For best results, start 1–2 days before you want to serve it to allow enough time to make the base, churn it, and freeze. For tips on making homemade ice cream, see page 189.

MAKES ABOUT 1 QUART

10 ounces (about 1 pint) fresh strawberries, hulled (or 9 ounces frozen strawberries)

1 cup granulated sugar, divided

Juice of ½ lemon, freshly squeezed (about 1 tablespoon)

2 cups heavy cream, divided

2 large egg yolks

Remove the tops from the strawberries and slice. Combine them with ¼ cup of the sugar and the lemon juice in a small bowl. Cover and refrigerate at least 1 hour.

Add 1 cup of cream to a large bowl. Set a strainer over the bowl and place near the stove.

In a medium saucepan off heat, whisk the yolks, then slowly whisk in the remaining 1 cup of cream. Stir in the remaining ¾ cup sugar. Cook over medium heat, stirring constantly with a wooden spoon, until it comes to a bare simmer, 5–8 minutes. Pour the hot mixture into the strainer bowl. Remove the strainer.

Puree the strawberry mixture in a blender or food processor until smooth (or you can keep it somewhat chunky if you prefer). Measure out 1 cup of strawberry puree and stir it into the ice cream mixture. Chill, covered, in the refrigerator until cold, 4–6 hours or overnight.

Freeze in an ice cream maker according to the manufacturer's instructions, then transfer to a freezer-safe container and freeze until firm, 6–8 hours. Store in the freezer for up to 1 month.

Note: For instructions on how to make ice cream without a machine, see page 190.

Variations

Easy No-Cook Strawberry: Macerate and puree the strawberries. Replace the egg yolks with 2 whole eggs (preferably pasteurized, since they will be raw). Whisk the eggs in a large bowl for 1–2 minutes until frothy. Whisk in the remaining ¾ cup sugar. Continue to whisk 1–2 minutes more until light-colored and thickened. Stir in the strawberry puree and cream. Proceed to churning. (For an egg-free alternative, just mix everything together and churn.)

Strawberry Basil: Steep a sprig of basil in the ice cream base as it comes to a simmer, then strain it out.

Rhode Island Coffee Ice Cream

Rhode Islanders love their coffee milk—a tall glass of milk flavored with coffee syrup. Coffee also happens to be one of my favorite ice cream flavors and one that's easily re-created at home. You don't need coffee syrup to make ice cream—you'll get great results with instant espresso powder or Starbuck's Italian Roast Via packets. But you can use the syrup to make terrific frappes or cabinets, as they're called in Rhode Island (page 205). For best results, start the day before you want to serve the ice cream to allow enough time to make the base, churn it, and freeze. For tips on making homemade ice cream, see page 189.

MAKES ABOUT 1 QUART

2 cups heavy cream, divided

2 large egg yolks

1 cup milk (preferably whole, but not skim)

¾ cup granulated sugar

2 tablespoons instant espresso powder (or your favorite instant coffee, large crystals ground with a mortar and pestle)

½ teaspoon vanilla extract

Add 1 cup of cream to a large bowl. Set a strainer over the bowl and place near the stove.

In a medium saucepan off heat, whisk the yolks, then slowly whisk in the milk. Gradually whisk in the sugar. Stir in the remaining 1 cup of cream. Cook over medium heat, stirring constantly with a wooden spoon, until it comes to a bare simmer, 5–8 minutes.

Remove the pan from the heat and whisk in the instant espresso powder (it doesn't have to be completely dissolved, as the churning process will take care of any stubborn lumps).

Pour the hot mixture into the strainer bowl. Remove the strainer and stir in the vanilla. Chill, covered, in the refrigerator until cold, 4–6 hours or overnight.

Freeze in an ice cream maker according to the manufacturer's instructions, then transfer to a freezer-safe container and freeze until firm, 6–8 hours. Store in the freezer for up to 1 month.

Note: For instructions on how to make ice cream without a machine, see page 190.

Variations

Easy No-Cook Coffee: Replace the egg yolks with 2 whole eggs (preferably pasteurized, since they will be raw). In a large bowl, whisk the eggs for 1–2 minutes until frothy. Whisk in the sugar. Continue to whisk 1–2 minutes more until light-colored and thickened. Add the espresso powder to the milk and whisk well, then slowly whisk it into the egg mixture. Stir in the vanilla and cream. Proceed to churning. (For an egg-free alternative, just mix everything together and churn.)

Coffee Hazelnut: Add ½ cup chopped toasted hazelnuts during the last minute of churning.

Coffee Ice Cream Sandwich: To replicate this popular flavor by Toscanini's Ice Cream in Cambridge, Massachusetts, chop 3 ice cream sandwiches into small pieces and fold them into the churned ice cream before freezing.

Vermont Maple Ice Cream

The secret to this super-simple ice cream is real maple sugar. It's not cheap, but the results will wow the true maple lover. If you can't find maple sugar at your local supermarket, you can order it online (I like Coombs Family Farms in Brattleboro, Vermont). Finely ground maple sugar dissolves much faster, but if your maple sugar is very coarse, you can run it through a food processor for a few minutes until powdery (run the kitchen fan to clear the dust). Or, if you prefer, you can sub ¾ cup of maple syrup (the darker, the better) for the maple sugar, but omit the milk entirely to balance out the extra water content. See the variation below for soft-serve Maple Creemees for a taste of Vermont. For best results, start the day before you want to serve the ice cream to allow enough time to make the base, churn it, and freeze. For tips on making homemade ice cream, see page 189.

MAKES ABOUT 1 QUART

2 cups heavy cream, divided

2 large egg yolks

1 cup milk (preferably whole, but not skim)

¾ cup finely ground maple sugar

Add 1 cup of the cream to a large bowl. Set a strainer over the bowl and place near the stove.

In a medium saucepan off heat, whisk the yolks, then slowly whisk in the milk. Gradually whisk in the maple sugar. Stir in the remaining 1 cup of cream. Cook over medium heat, stirring constantly with a wooden spoon, until it comes to a bare simmer, 5–8 minutes.

Pour the hot mixture into the strainer bowl. Remove the strainer. Chill, covered, in the refrigerator until cold, 4–6 hours or overnight.

Freeze in an ice cream maker according to the manufacturer's instructions, then transfer to a freezer-safe container and freeze until firm, 6–8 hours. Store in the freezer for up to 1 month.

Note: For instructions on how to make ice cream without a machine, see page 190.

Variations

Vermont Maple Creemees: Replace the egg yolks with 2 whole eggs (preferably pasteurized, since they will be raw). In a large bowl, whisk the eggs for 1–2 minutes until frothy. Whisk in the maple sugar. Continue to whisk 1–2 minutes more until light-colored and thickened. Add the milk and whisk well. Stir in the cream. Freeze in an ice cream maker according to the manufacturer's instructions. Serve right away or spoon into a freezer-safe container and freeze just 1–2 hours. The ice cream should be soft-serve consistency. You can use a pastry bag fitted with a large star tip to dispense the ice cream, but work quickly—it melts fast!

Maple Walnut: Stir ¾ cup coarsely chopped walnuts into the churned ice cream and freeze until firm.

Maple Bacon: Got leftover bacon? Dice 3 strips of cooked bacon as small as you reasonably can. (To make a quick batch in the microwave, set the bacon slices on a paper towel–lined plate, cover with a few more paper towels, and heat on high about 3 minutes, checking often until done.) Stir in the diced bacon after churning and freeze until firm.

Maine Buttermilk and Sea Salt Ice Cream

Here's another option besides vanilla to serve with your seasonal fruit pies and crisps. This one is particularly great served with sliced fresh peaches or nectarines, or your favorite farmers' market blackberry jam. For the purest flavor, use real buttermilk, like Kate's from Arundel, Maine, the natural by-product of the butter-making process. If you can't get your hands on fresh buttermilk, you can substitute crème fraîche (try Vermont Creamery). In that case, use 4 ounces of crème fraîche, reduce the heavy cream to 1½ cups, and add 1 cup of milk. For best results, start the day before you want to serve it to allow enough time to make the base, churn it, and freeze. For tips on making homemade ice cream, see page 189.

MAKES ABOUT 1 QUART

¾ cup real buttermilk

2 large egg yolks

2 cups heavy cream

¾ cup granulated sugar

¼ teaspoon fine sea salt

Add the buttermilk to a large bowl. Set a strainer over the bowl and place near the stove.

In a medium saucepan off heat, whisk the yolks, then slowly whisk in the cream. Stir in the sugar and salt. Cook over medium heat, stirring constantly with a wooden spoon, until it comes to a bare simmer, 5–8 minutes. Pour the hot mixture into the strainer bowl. Remove the strainer. Chill, covered, in the refrigerator until cold, 4–6 hours or overnight.

Freeze in an ice cream maker according to the manufacturer's instructions, then transfer to a freezer-safe container and freeze until firm, 6–8 hours. Store in the freezer for up to 1 month.

Note: For instructions on how to make ice cream without a machine, see page 190.

Variation

Easy No-Cook Buttermilk: Replace the egg yolks with 2 whole eggs (preferably pasteurized, since they will be raw). In a large bowl, whisk the eggs for 1–2 minutes until frothy. Whisk in the sugar. Continue to whisk 1–2 minutes more until light-colored and thickened. Whisk in the buttermilk and salt. Stir in the cream. Proceed to churning. (For an egg-free alternative, just mix everything together and churn.)

Frappes

Don't bother asking for a frappe outside of New England—you'll be met with befuddled stares. Frappes (pronounced "fraps," not "frap-PAYS") are what the rest of the country calls milk shakes: a thick, creamy frozen beverage made with ice cream, milk, and flavored syrup. But if you ask for a milk shake here in New England, you'll receive a glass of frothy milk flavored with syrup and that's it. No ice cream. And you surely want ice cream, don't you?

The word "frappe," French in origin, means "to beat," which accurately describes the mixing process involved. The word most likely originated from the large French-Canadian population in the area. Frappes are also called "frosts" in western Massachusetts, and "cabinets" in Rhode Island and parts of Connecticut (the cabinet is where you store the blender, after all).

The secret to a great-tasting frappe, besides the all-important ice cream, is not to skimp on the syrup. It prevents the milk from diluting the flavor of the ice cream. For vanilla and maple, it's easy. Just add more vanilla extract or maple syrup. For chocolate, strawberry, or coffee, you'll need to make or buy a flavor booster to get that extra flavor. For old-time nostalgia, you can make any of the below flavors "malted" by blending 2–3 tablespoons malted milk powder (like Horlick's or Carnation) in the milk before adding the ice cream and syrup.

Stick blenders work great for individual frappes, but regular blenders will save you time for a group. Each recipe below is for a single large serving, which makes it easy to scale up. Depending on the size of your ice cream scoops, you may need to add more milk. (Remember not to fill your blender more than ¾ of the way up.)

Vanilla

Add 3 medium scoops of Connecticut Valley Vanilla Ice Cream (page 193), ¼ cup milk, and ½ teaspoon vanilla extract to a blender. Blend on high until pourable. Add more milk as needed.

Chocolate

Add 3 medium scoops of Beantown Chocolate Ice Cream (page 195), ¼ cup milk, and 2 tablespoons Hot Fudge (page 220) or your favorite store-bought chocolate syrup to a blender. Blend on high until pourable. Add more milk as needed.

Strawberry

Add 3 medium scoops of New Hampshire Strawberry Ice Cream (page 197), ¼ cup milk, and 2 tablespoons strawberry syrup (see below) to a blender. Blend on high until pourable. Add more milk as needed.

To make your own strawberry syrup, slice 1 pound of hulled strawberries and add to a small saucepan with ¾ cup water. Bring to a boil. Simmer 15 minutes. Strain through a fine-mesh sieve (don't press on the fruits, which will make the syrup cloudy—just let it sit for 10 minutes, gently stirring the fruit occasionally). Discard the fruit. Measure the liquid in a measuring cup. Add it back to the pot with an equal amount of granulated sugar. Bring to a boil, stirring frequently. Simmer 1–2 minutes until thick and syrupy. Let cool, then chill in the refrigerator, covered, for up to 3 weeks.

Coffee

Add 3 medium scoops Rhode Island Coffee Ice Cream (page 200), ¼ cup milk, and 2 tablespoons cold coffee or coffee syrup. Blend on high until pourable. Add more milk as needed.

Due to the popularity of coffee milk, there are several brands of coffee syrup available for purchase in Rhode Island and beyond, including Autocrat, Eclipse, Coffee Time, and my personal favorite, Dave's. Look for them at the supermarket where you'd find Hershey's chocolate syrup, or you can purchase them online.

Maple

Add 3 medium scoops of Vermont Maple Ice Cream (page 202), ¼ cup milk, and 2 tablespoons pure maple syrup (the darker, the better). Blend on high until pourable. Add more milk as needed.

Mocha

Add 3 medium scoops of Mocha Chip Ice Cream (page 214)—made without the chips—to a blender. Or add your favorite ratio of Beantown Chocolate Ice Cream (page 195) and Rhode Island Coffee Ice Cream (page 200). Add ¼ cup milk, 1 tablespoon Hot Fudge (page 220) or store-bought chocolate syrup, and 1 tablespoon cold coffee or store-bought coffee syrup. Blend on high until pourable. Add more milk as needed.

Mint Chocolate Chip Ice Cream

Growing up outside of Boston, one of my favorite treats was a sugar cone with mint chocolate chip ice cream and jimmies from Brigham's in the South Shore Plaza. This is my homemade version. It's a good use for all that runaway mint that's taken over your garden by midsummer. Instead of chocolate chips, which can freeze hard, I melt dark chocolate and drizzle it into the churned ice cream to create a delicate stracciatella ("little shreds"). This ice cream has a very subtle, naturally green hue, but feel free to take it up a notch with some green food coloring. If you don't have fresh mint leaves, you can skip the steeping process and add 1 teaspoon spearmint extract or mint extract that contains some amount of spearmint oil (save the pure peppermint extract for the Peppermint Stick Ice Cream on page 174). For best results, start 1–2 days before you want to serve it to allow enough time to make the base, churn it, and freeze. For tips on making homemade ice cream, see page 189.

MAKES ABOUT 1 QUART

- 1 cup fresh mint leaves, loosely packed (about 30–40 leaves)
- 1½ cups milk (preferably whole, but not skim)
- 1½ cups heavy cream, divided
- 2 large egg yolks
- ¾ cup granulated sugar
- 3 ounces bittersweet chocolate, chopped (not chips)

Tear the mint leaves into smaller pieces and add them to a small saucepan with the milk. Heat the milk until steaming (no need to boil). Remove the pot from the heat, stir, and let steep until cool. Pour into a jar, cover, and refrigerate until cold, at least 3 hours or overnight. Strain the mixture into a small bowl and discard the leaves.

Add 1 cup of cream to a large bowl. Set a strainer over the bowl and place near the stove.

In a medium saucepan off heat, whisk the yolks, then slowly whisk in the minty milk. Whisk in the sugar. Stir in the remaining ½ cup of cream. Cook over medium heat, stirring constantly with a wooden spoon, until it comes to a bare simmer, 5–8 minutes.

Remove the pan from the heat. Pour the hot mixture into the nested sieve. Remove the sieve. (If using mint extract instead of fresh mint, add it here.) Chill, covered, in the refrigerator until cold, 4–6 hours or overnight.

Freeze in an ice cream maker according to the manufacturer's instructions. Towards the end of the churning, heat the chopped chocolate in the microwave (stirring every 30 seconds or so) or on top of a double boiler (you can improvise your own by setting a metal bowl on top of a small saucepan

that contains an inch of simmering water). Stir the chocolate until melted and smooth, 1–2 minutes. It should still be warm when the ice cream is done churning. When transferring the churned ice cream to a freezer-safe container, alternate layers of ice cream with light drizzles of chocolate, stirring vigorously with a fork as you go to break up the cooling ribbons of chocolate into little chips.

Set in the freezer until firm, 6–8 hours. Store in the freezer for up to 1 month.

Note: For instructions on how to make ice cream without a machine, see page 190.

Variation

Easy No-Cook Version: Replace the egg yolks with 2 whole eggs (preferably pasteurized, since they will be raw). Whisk the eggs in a large bowl for 1–2 minutes until very frothy. Whisk in the sugar. Continue to whisk 1–2 minutes more until light-colored and thickened. Whisk in the milk and 1 teaspoon mint extract. Stir in the cream. Proceed to churning. (You can also leave the eggs out entirely and just mix everything together before churning.)

Pecan Penuche Ice Cream

Butter pecan is the more traditional flavor to find on ice cream boards across New England, but I was so inspired by the Pecan Penuche offered by Four Seas Ice Cream in Centerville, Cape Cod, I decided to try my hand at it. The praline-ish flavor is delightfully reminiscent of the popular New England brown sugar fudge. You want fresh, very sweet nuts for this recipe, not ones that have been sitting around for months/years. Store your unused nuts in the freezer so they stay fresh. I prefer raw nuts, but you can toast them first if you prefer. Just spread them out on a sheet pan and bake at 350°F until fragrant and starting to brown, 7–10 minutes, or toss in a dry sauté pan over medium heat for about 5 minutes. If you're a purist, you can turn this recipe into Butter Pecan by substituting white granulated sugar for the brown sugar, doubling the salt, and adding a full stick of melted, unsalted butter to the custard base. For best results, start the day before you want to serve it to allow enough time to make the base, churn, and freeze it. For tips on making homemade ice cream, see page 189.

1½ cups heavy cream, divided

2 large egg yolks

1 cup milk (preferably whole, but not skim)

¾ cup dark brown sugar, packed

¼ teaspoon salt

2 tablespoons unsalted butter

1 teaspoon vanilla extract

1 cup chopped pecans

Add ½ cup of cream to a large bowl. Set a strainer over the bowl and place near the stove.

In a medium saucepan off heat, whisk the yolks, then slowly whisk in the milk. Whisk in the brown sugar. Stir in the remaining 1 cup of cream and the salt. Cook over medium heat, stirring constantly with a wooden spoon, until it comes to a bare simmer, 5–8 minutes.

Remove the pan from the heat and add the butter, stirring until melted. Pour the hot mixture into the strainer bowl. Remove the strainer and stir in the vanilla. Chill, covered, in the refrigerator until cold, 4–6 hours or overnight.

Freeze in an ice cream maker according to the manufacturer's instructions. Stir in the pecans after the churning is complete. Transfer to a freezer-safe container and freeze until firm, 6–8 hours. Store in the freezer for up to 1 month.

Note: For instructions on how to make ice cream without a machine, see page 190.

Variation

Easy No-Cook Version: Replace the egg yolks with 2 whole eggs (preferably pasteurized, since they will be raw). Whisk the eggs in a large bowl for 1–2 minutes until frothy. Whisk in the brown sugar and salt. Continue to whisk 1–2 minutes more until light-colored and thickened. Melt the butter and mix it in. Whisk in the milk and vanilla. Stir in the cream. Proceed to churning. (You can also leave the eggs out entirely and just mix everything together before churning.)

Grape-Nuts Ice Cream

Grape-Nuts is one of the nation's oldest packaged cereals, dating back to 1898. Containing neither grapes nor nuts, it instead features an amalgam of malted barley and whole wheat flour, baked to a hearty crunch. It's popular with back-to-the-landers, health fanatics, the elderly, and me. I love how the crunchy little nuggets soften and mellow into malty, toothsome perfection. A little bit of malted milk powder sweetens the deal. If you can't find malted milk powder at the grocery store, you can order it online or just leave it out. For best results, start the day before you want to serve it to allow enough time to make the base, churn, and freeze it. For tips on making homemade ice cream, see page 189.

2 cups heavy cream, divided

2 large egg yolks

1 cup milk (preferably whole, but not skim)

⅔ cup granulated sugar

2 heaping tablespoons malted milk powder, like Horlick's or Carnation (optional)

¾ cup Grape-Nuts cereal

Add 1 cup of cream to a large bowl. Set a standard mesh strainer over the bowl and place near the stove.

In a medium saucepan off heat, whisk the yolks, then slowly whisk in the milk. Whisk in the sugar. Stir in the remaining 1 cup of cream. Cook over medium heat, stirring constantly with a wooden spoon, until it comes to a bare simmer, 5–8 minutes.

Remove the pot from the heat and whisk in the malted milk powder until dissolved. Pour the hot mixture into the strainer bowl. Remove the strainer. Chill, covered, in the refrigerator until cold, 4–6 hours or overnight.

Freeze in an ice cream maker according to the manufacturer's instructions. Add the Grape-Nuts during the last minute of churning or stir in the Grape-Nuts after churning is complete. Transfer to a freezer-safe container and freeze until firm, 6–8 hours. Store in the freezer for up to 1 month.

Note: For instructions on how to make ice cream without a machine, see page 190.

Variation

Easy No-Cook Version: Replace the egg yolks with 2 whole eggs (preferably pasteurized, since they will be raw). Whisk the eggs in a large bowl for 1–2 minutes until frothy. Whisk in the sugar. Continue to whisk 1–2 minutes more until light-colored and thickened. Whisk in the milk and malted milk powder. Stir in the cream. Proceed to churning. (You can also leave the eggs out entirely and just mix everything together before churning.)

Mocha Chip Ice Cream

This delectable combination of chocolate and coffee has long been a popular ice cream flavor in New England, though the particular ratio of chocolate to coffee was hotly debated among my tasters. Not enough chocolate said one half. Not enough coffee said the other. I've concluded it's highly personal, so feel free to tweak the flavors to your liking. Rather than using chocolate chips, I've opted for the Italian method of ribboning warm melted chocolate into the churned ice cream to create delicate chips, known as stracciatella *("little shreds"). Try to use block chocolate instead of chocolate chips—it drizzles more finely and creates a better mouth-feel in the freezer. If you can't find instant espresso powder in the coffee section of your supermarket, you can use strong instant coffee like Starbucks Via. Note that if your instant coffee comes in large granules, you should first grind them in a mortar and pestle or food processor until powdery so they dissolve properly. For best results, start the day before you want to serve it to allow enough time to make the base, churn, and freeze it. For tips on making homemade ice cream, see page 189.*

MAKES ABOUT 1 QUART

- 1¾ cups heavy cream, divided
- 2 large egg yolks
- 1 cup milk (preferably whole, but not skim)
- ¾ cup granulated sugar
- Pinch of salt
- 2 tablespoons unsweetened cocoa powder, preferably Dutch-process
- 1 tablespoon instant espresso powder or instant coffee powder
- 1 teaspoon vanilla extract
- 4 ounces bittersweet chocolate, chopped (not chips)

Add 1 cup of cream to a large bowl. Set a fine-mesh sieve over the bowl and place near the stove.

In a medium saucepan off heat, whisk the yolks, then slowly whisk in the milk. Whisk in the sugar and salt. Stir in the remaining ¾ cup of cream. Cook over medium heat, stirring constantly with a wooden spoon, until it comes to a bare simmer, 5–8 minutes.

Remove the pan from the heat and whisk in the cocoa and instant espresso powder. Pour the hot mixture through the sieve into the bowl with the cream. Remove the sieve and stir in the vanilla. Chill, covered, in the refrigerator until cold, 4–6 hours or overnight.

Freeze in an ice cream maker according to the manufacturer's instructions. Towards the end of the churning, heat the chopped chocolate in the microwave (stirring every 30 seconds or so) or on top of a double boiler (you can improvise your own by setting a metal bowl on top of a small saucepan containing an inch of simmering water). Stir the chocolate until melted and smooth, 1–2 minutes. It should still be warm when the ice cream is done churning. When transferring the churned ice cream to a freezer-safe container, alternate layers of ice cream with light drizzles of chocolate, stirring vigorously with a fork as you go to break up the cooling ribbons of chocolate into little chips.

Set in the freezer until firm, 6–8 hours. Store in the freezer for up to 1 month.

Note: For instructions on how to make ice cream without a machine, see page 190.

Variation

Easy No-Cook Version: Replace the egg yolks with 2 whole eggs (preferably pasteurized, since they will be raw). Whisk the eggs in a large bowl for 1–2 minutes until frothy. Whisk in the sugar and salt. Continue to whisk 1–2 minutes more until light-colored and thickened. Whisk in the milk and vanilla. Whisk in the cocoa powder and espresso powder until dissolved. Stir in the cream. Proceed to churning. (You can also leave the eggs out entirely and just mix everything together before churning.)

Landslide Ice Cream

This flavor was created by my youngest son, who was 12 when he dreamed up the idea for chocolate peanut butter ice cream with a marshmallow swirl. Even the name was his creation. We tried a few variations on the concept, and this was his favorite, with little pockets of peanut butter hidden away. Note: This is an uncooked ice cream, so feel free to leave out the eggs if you can't find pasteurized. While I think natural peanut butter like Massachusetts-based Teddie, has better flavor, you can substitute processed peanut butter instead. Just reduce the brown sugar in the ice cream to ⅔ cup to offset the added sweeteners, and omit the brown sugar and water for the peanut butter pockets.

MAKES ABOUT 1½ QUARTS

For the ice cream:

2 large pasteurized eggs

¾ cup light brown sugar, firmly packed

½ cup natural salted smooth peanut butter

½ cup semisweet chocolate chips

1 teaspoon vanilla extract

3 tablespoons unsweetened cocoa powder

1 cup milk (preferably whole, but not skim)

2 cups heavy cream

½ cup Marshmallow Fluff

For the peanut butter pockets:

¼ cup natural salted smooth peanut butter

2 tablespoons light brown sugar, firmly packed

1 tablespoon hot water

In a large bowl, whisk the eggs and brown sugar together, 1–2 minutes. Mix in the peanut butter, and whisk 1 minute more.

In a small, microwave safe bowl, melt the chocolate chips in short 30-second bursts on high power, stirring in between each burst until melted, 2–3 minutes. Stir the melted chocolate and vanilla into the sugar mixture with a wooden spoon. Mixture will be very thick. Add the cocoa powder, and slowly whisk in half of the milk to loosen. Add the rest of the milk and the cream. Stir until combined.

Pour the mixture into an ice cream machine and follow the manufacturer's instructions. While the ice cream is processing, stir together the peanut butter, brown sugar, and hot water in a small bowl. Mixture should be thick, but hold its shape.

Spoon the ice cream mixture into a freezer-safe container in layers. Between each layer, add dollops of Marshmallow Fluff and teaspoon-sized balls of the peanut butter mixture. Freeze until firm, 4–6 hours. Store in the freezer for up to 1 month.

Note: For instructions on how to make ice cream without a machine, see page 190.

Nutella Crunch Ice Cream

We always have a jar of Nutella in the house and a box of Grape-Nuts in the pantry. And one day, a new ice cream mash-up was born. The combination reminds me of Ferrero Rocher candies. If you're not a fan of Grape-Nuts, feel free to substitute ½ cup chopped toasted hazelnuts instead. For best results, start the day before you want to serve it to allow enough time to make the base, churn, and freeze it. For tips on making homemade ice cream, see page 189.

MAKES ABOUT 1½ QUARTS

1½ cups heavy cream, divided

2 large egg yolks

¾ cup milk (preferably whole, but not skim)

¼ cup granulated sugar

¾ cup Nutella, well-stirred

½ teaspoon vanilla extract

¾ cup Grape-Nuts cereal

Add ¾ cup of the cream to a large bowl. Set a strainer in the bowl and place near the stove.

In a medium saucepan off heat, whisk the yolks, then slowly whisk in the milk. Whisk in the sugar. Stir in the remaining ¾ cup cream. Cook over medium heat, stirring constantly with a wooden spoon, until it comes to a bare simmer, 5–8 minutes.

Remove the pot from the heat and pour the hot mixture into the strainer bowl. Remove the strainer. Whisk in the Nutella until dissolved. Stir in the vanilla. Chill, covered, in the refrigerator until cold, 4–6 hours or overnight.

Freeze in an ice cream maker according to the manufacturer's instructions. Stir in the Grape-Nuts after churning is complete. Transfer to a freezer-safe container and freeze until firm, 6–8 hours. Store in the freezer for up to 1 month.

Note: For instructions on how to make ice cream without a machine, see page 190.

Variation

Easy No-Cook Version: Replace the egg yolks with 2 whole eggs (preferably pasteurized, as they will be raw) and whisk in a large bowl for 1–2 minutes until frothy. Whisk in the sugar. Continue to whisk 1–2 minutes more until light-colored and thickened. Add the Nutella and vanilla. Mix well. Whisk in the milk, then the cream. Proceed to churning. (You can also leave the eggs out entirely and just mix everything together except the Grape-Nuts before churning.)

S'Mores Ice Cream

We love to explore the many beautiful campgrounds throughout New England in the spring and fall, when it's not too hot. In that spirit, here's my version of everyone's favorite campfire treat, minus the campfire. As much as I love chocolate and marshmallow, this graham cracker ice cream was a delicious surprise. Turns out, this trio is just as good cold and frosty as it is warm and gooey. For best results, start the day before you want to serve it to allow enough time to make the base, churn, and freeze it. For tips on making homemade ice cream, see page 189.

MAKES ABOUT 1½ QUARTS

9 honey graham crackers (1 sleeve)

1 cup milk (preferably whole, but not skim)

2 large egg yolks

2 cups heavy cream, plus ¼ cup for the chocolate swirl

⅓ cup granulated sugar

6 ounces milk chocolate chips or Hershey bars (broken up into small pieces)

⅓ cup Marshmallow Fluff, divided

1½ cup mini-marshmallows (optional)

Crumble the graham crackers into smallish pieces in a medium bowl and cover with milk. Let soak (the graham crackers will start to disintegrate).

In a medium saucepan off heat, whisk the yolks, then slowly whisk in the cream. Whisk in the sugar. Cook over medium heat, stirring constantly with a wooden spoon, until it comes to a bare simmer, 5–8 minutes.

Remove the pan from the heat. Set a fine-mesh sieve over the bowl of soggy graham crackers. Pour the hot mixture through the sieve. Remove the sieve and stir well. Chill, covered, in the refrigerator until cold, 4–6 hours or overnight (the graham crackers will continue to disintegrate).

Freeze in an ice cream maker according to the manufacturer's instructions.

Meanwhile, add the chocolate and ¼ cup cream to a small microwave-safe bowl. Microwave on medium-high in 20-second bursts, stirring with a fork in between, until the chocolate mixture is melted and smooth. While the mixture is still warm, add 3 tablespoons Marshmallow Fluff, but only partially mix it in, keeping it streaky. Let cool while the ice cream finishes churning.

Transfer the churned ice cream into a freezer-safe container, layering with generous amounts of chocolate-marshmallow swirl. Add dollops of the remaining Marshmallow Fluff as you go. Top with mini-marshmallows if desired.

Freeze until firm, 6–8 hours. Store in the freezer for up to 1 month.

Note: For instructions on how to make ice cream without a machine, see page 190.

Variation

Up Your Game: If you happen to have a kitchen torch, consider adding a little fire to the equation. Layer your ice cream components in a metal loaf pan before freezing, and top with 1½ cups marshmallows (large or mini). Cover tightly and freeze as instructed. When ready to serve, remove the plastic wrap and toast the marshmallows with a kitchen torch until they turn toasty brown and blacken in spots. Serve immediately.

Hot Fudge Sauce

In our house, we often find ourselves melting chocolate and cream in the microwave (ganache, essentially) to pour over ice cream. But, for this book, I wanted to come up with a proper hot fudge sauce—one that's glossy, ribbons thickly, and has that traditional New England chew. I also didn't want to use corn syrup, which added an extra challenge. This rich and fudgy bittersweet elixir hit all the right notes. Be extra careful not to introduce any undissolved sugar crystals into your sauce or it will get grainy over time (I've provided tips in the instructions for how to avoid this). A good quality, high-fat, Dutch-process cocoa makes a difference here, ensuring the sauce has a deep, chocolaty flavor without being too acidic. That said, you can substitute regular unsweetened cocoa powder if you wish. For a thinner chocolate sauce, reduce the cooking time by 25%.

MAKES ABOUT 2 CUPS

1¼ cups water

1½ cups granulated sugar

4 tablespoons unsalted butter

½ cup unsweetened Dutch-process cocoa powder, sifted

½ teaspoon fine sea salt

4 ounces bittersweet chopped chocolate or ⅔ cup bittersweet chocolate chips

1 teaspoon vanilla extract

2 tablespoons heavy cream

In a small heavy-bottomed saucepan, heat the water, sugar, and butter over medium-low heat, stirring occasionally, until the butter melts. Whisk in the cocoa powder and salt. Cook, whisking constantly, until bubbles form around the edges.

Generously brush the sides of the pan with water to remove any undissolved sugar crystals hiding in the chocolate residue. Reduce the heat to low and simmer about 10 minutes, without stirring, until the mixture thickens. (If your pan is very small, keep an eye on it so the mixture doesn't boil over.)

Fetch a clean wooden spoon (this is important so you don't reintroduce sugar crystals from the previous step). Stir in the chocolate chips and vanilla until melted. Simmer on low, stirring occasionally, 5–10 minutes more until it thickly coats the back of the spoon and is reduced to less than 2 cups.

Remove the pan from the heat and let cool to warm room temperature. Stir in the cream, 1 tablespoon at a time, until you reach your desired consistency (for me, that's thin enough to pour fluidly but thick enough to ribbon nicely over cold ice cream).

Transfer to a pint jar and let cool completely. Hot fudge can be stored, covered, in the refrigerator for 1–2 weeks. To reheat, remove the lid and gently heat in the microwave in 15-second increments at 50% power, stirring in between, just until pourable.

Ice Cream Sundaes

Here are a few suggestions for pairing ice cream with toppings and bakeshop treats to create stellar sundaes all year round:

Brownie Sundae

Always a classic, top the Salted + Malted Brownies (page 24) with Connecticut Valley Vanilla Ice Cream (page 193) or Peppermint Stick Ice Cream (page 174), Hot Fudge Sauce (page 220), Whipped Cream (page 229), and a Brandied Cherry (page 71).

Butterscotch Bliss Sundae

Serve Connecticut Valley Vanilla Ice Cream (page 193) or Maine Buttermilk and Sea Salt Ice Cream (page 204) over Butterscotch Blondies (page 176) and top with Butterscotch Sauce (page 227) or Salted Caramel Sauce (page 224), Whipped Cream (page 229), and a Brandied Cherry (page 71).

Apple Orchard Sundae

Serve slices of Apple Cider Doughnut Cake (page 107) with Connecticut Valley Vanilla Ice Cream (page 193) or Maine Buttermilk and Sea Salt Ice Cream (page 204), and top with Salted Caramel Sauce (page 224), Whipped Cream (page 229), and a Brandied Cherry (page 71).

Fruit Pie Sundae

Top Connecticut Valley Vanilla Ice Cream (page 193) or Maine Buttermilk and Sea Salt Ice Cream (page 204) with Strawberry Rhubarb Sauce (page 39), Blueberry Sauce (page 83), or Peach Ginger Compote (page 84), and crumble Pie Crisps on top (page 78).

Classic Banana Split

In an oblong dish, line up a scoop each of Beantown Chocolate Ice Cream (page 195), Connecticut Valley Vanilla Ice Cream (page 193), and New Hampshire Strawberry Ice Cream (page 197). Peel and slice a banana lengthwise and lay each half along each side. Top with your choice of Hot Fudge (page

220), Balsamic Strawberry Sauce (page 225), Salted Caramel Sauce (page 224), or Butterscotch Sauce (page 227). Add Whipped Cream (page 229), a sprinkling of chopped walnuts if desired, and 3 Brandied Cherries (page 71).

Brazilian Combo

Cabot's in Newton, Massachusetts, serves an enormous sundae with these approximate flavor combinations: one scoop each of Rhode Island Coffee Ice Cream (page 200), Maple Walnut Ice Cream (page 203), Pecan Penuche Ice Cream (page 210), and Connecticut Valley Vanilla Ice Cream (page 193) paired with one or more sauces like Hot Fudge (page 220), Salted Caramel (page 224), Butterscotch (page 227), or Peanut Butter (page 228). Finish with Whipped Cream (page 229) and 4 Brandied Cherries (page 71).

Reese's Pieces Sundae

Inspired by its counterpart at Friendly's, serve two scoops of Connecticut Valley Vanilla Ice Cream (page 193) with Hot Fudge Sauce (page 220), Peanut Butter Topping (page 228), and Old-Fashioned Marshmallow Sauce (page 229). Add Whipped Cream (page 229), Reese's Pieces, sprinkles, and a Brandied Cherry (page 71).

Green Monster Sundae

Gifford's in Maine makes a Red Sox–themed sundae with Mint Chocolate Chip Ice Cream (page 207) topped with Hot Fudge Sauce (page 220), Whipped Cream (page 229), and chocolate sprinkles.

Salted Caramel Sauce

Of all the recipes I've tested for this book, this is the one I can't keep in the house because I will eat it all right out of the jar until it's gone. My loss is your gain. Use this caramel sauce for sundaes like the Apple Orchard Sundae, Classic Banana Split (page 222), or Brazilian Combo (page 223), or drizzled over Caramel Apple Tarts (page 93). It's also delightful for dipping fresh apple slices.

MAKES 1½ CUPS

1 cup granulated sugar

4 tablespoons unsalted butter, cut into quarters

¾ cup heavy cream

1 teaspoon kosher salt or fine sea salt

Add the sugar to a medium heavy-bottomed saucepan, and shake to evenly disperse the sugar across the bottom of the pan. Cook over medium-low heat without stirring until the sugar starts to melt. Continue cooking, stirring only occasionally for even cooking, until all the sugar is melted and the mixture turns a deep amber color. Remove the pan from the heat and add the butter, stirring until melted. Add the cream and salt. Over low heat, stir to dissolve any hardened caramel in the pot until smooth, 3–5 minutes. Pour into a pint jar and let cool. To store, cover and refrigerate for up to 1 month. To serve, remove the lid and gently reheat in the microwave in short bursts, stirring in between, until warm and pourable.

Balsamic Strawberry Sauce

By itself, this strawberry sauce might seem a tad heavy on the balsamic, but, trust me, the acidity and extra fruitiness is divine over vanilla ice cream—even chocolate! If you don't have balsamic vinegar, you can sub in red or white wine vinegar, even Champagne vinegar. Or just keep to the classics by adding a small squeeze of lemon juice instead.

MAKES 2½ CUPS

1 quart fresh strawberries or 1½ pounds frozen
½ cup granulated sugar
2 tablespoons balsamic vinegar
Pinch of salt

Hull and quarter the strawberries if small (if large, cut into bite-sized pieces).

Combine the strawberries with the sugar in a small saucepan off heat and let sit 20 minutes until the strawberries start to release their juices.

Set the pot over medium heat and bring to a simmer. Lower the heat, add the vinegar, and continue simmering 3–5 minutes, stirring occasionally, until the strawberries soften (but still hold their shape) and the liquid thickens slightly and becomes syrupy. Remove from the heat and stir in the tiniest pinch of salt. Let cool.

Transfer to jars and store covered in the refrigerator until ready to serve. Serve over ice cream or Honey Cornmeal Cake (page 85).

Butterscotch Sauce

There's a fine line between butterscotch and salted caramel. Both use sugar, butter, cream, and salt to achieve an addictive, perfectly pourable ice cream topping. What's the difference? Caramel is made by melting and caramelizing white sugar (hence the name), while butterscotch builds on the molasses flavor of dark brown sugar, cooked just enough to coax out its inner complexity and boosted by a heavy hand with the vanilla. My version of butterscotch has an additional secret ingredient: buttermilk, which cuts the sweetness with its acidic tang. For best results, use real buttermilk left over from the butter-making process (like Kate's buttermilk in Maine) rather than substituting cultured or soured milk.

MAKES ABOUT 1¼ CUPS

2 tablespoons unsalted butter

1 cup dark brown sugar, firmly packed

¼ cup real buttermilk

½ cup heavy cream, warmed in the microwave

1 tablespoon vanilla extract

¾ teaspoon Maine sea salt (or ½ teaspoon table salt)

In a small heavy-bottomed saucepan, melt the butter over medium heat. Add the brown sugar and buttermilk, and stir with a wooden spoon. When it comes to a boil, reduce the heat to low and cook, stirring constantly, 4–5 minutes. Slowly whisk the warmed cream into the sugar mixture and cook for no more than 1 minute to keep the sauce nice and fluid when cooled (otherwise, you'll end up with candy). Remove the pot from the heat, stir in the vanilla and salt, and let cool. Pour into a half-pint jar and store in the refrigerator for 1–2 months (but it won't last that long). Spoon over ice cream cold or remove the lid and heat gently in the microwave 10–15 seconds.

Peanut Butter Topping

I don't know about anyone else, but I was addicted to the peanut butter sundae topping at Friendly's, the local restaurant chain founded in Springfield, Massachusetts, in 1935. The combination of hot fudge and salty, creamy peanut butter sauce over vanilla ice cream was salty, sweet, and divine. I make it primarily with creamy processed peanut butter because it holds the emulsion better, but then I stir in a bit of all-natural peanut butter for some texture and big peanutty flavor. For a dairy-free option, just omit the butter.

MAKES ABOUT 2 CUPS

½ cup granulated sugar

½ cup water

4 tablespoons unsalted butter

½ teaspoon fine sea salt

1 cup processed creamy peanut butter (like Jif)

2 tablespoons all-natural smooth peanut butter (like Teddie)

½ cup neutral oil, like peanut, vegetable, or canola

In a small saucepan over medium-low heat, stir together the sugar, water, butter, and salt until the sugar dissolves. Bring to a simmer, stirring occasionally, and let the mixture bubble over low heat for 1 minute. Remove from the heat and let cool to room temperature.

Add the two types of peanut butter to the bowl of a food processor or blender, and pulse briefly to mix. With the motor running, pour the oil through the feed tube in a slow and steady stream, scraping down the bottom and sides at least once. The mixture should look very thin.

After the oil is fully incorporated, pour the sugar syrup through the feed tube, with the motor running, in a slow and steady stream, mixing just until combined and scraping down the bowl as needed. The mixture should have thickened slightly but still be pourable—or at least ploppable. (Be warned that you need to add the oil first and the sugar syrup second for this recipe to work. If you reverse the order, the emulsion will break and you'll end up with an oily, sloshy mess.)

Store in the refrigerator in a covered pint jar for up to 2 weeks. Reheat gently in the microwave (without the lid) in 30-second increments at 50% power, stirring in between.

Tip: If using brands other than Jif and Teddie, you may need to adjust the amount of oil or peanut butter to get the perfect consistency, one that pours fluidly when warm but thickens a bit as it nestles up against cold ice cream. To thin it, you can mix in 1 (maybe 2) additional tablespoons of oil, if necessary, but much more and the sauce loses stability. To thicken it, mix in a bit more peanut butter a little at a time.

Old-Fashioned Marshmallow Sauce

One of the classic toppings of ice cream parlors of yore, this marshmallow sauce adds sweet, fluffy decadence to your ice cream sundae spread. Plus, it's incredibly easy to make.

SERVES 6-8

¼ cup granulated sugar
¼ cup water
4 ounces marshmallows
(cut into pieces if large)

Combine sugar and water in a small saucepan. Heat on medium, stirring occasionally, until simmering and the sugar is dissolved. Reduce the heat to low and stir in the marshmallows in four batches, letting each batch partially melt before adding the next. When the last batch is mostly melted, finish stirring off the heat until completely melted and smooth. Let cool slightly before using. To store, pour into a glass bowl or jar, cover, and refrigerate until ready to use. To reheat, remove the cover and microwave gently to reheat as needed.

Whipped Cream

While unsweetened whipped cream is acceptable and often preferable for very sweet desserts, I'm including this lightly sweetened version, which works well for ice cream sundaes and many other desserts in this book. If using an electric mixer, take care not to overbeat the cream. Take it too far and your whipped cream will end up speckled with little flecks of butter.

SERVES 4-6

1 cup cold heavy cream
1 tablespoon confectioner's sugar
Dribble of vanilla extract

Add the cream to a large bowl, preferably more deep than wide to reduce spattering. With an electric mixer or a whisk, whip the cream until bubbly, 5 seconds with a mixer and 20 seconds by hand. Add the sugar and vanilla and whip with an electric mixer on medium-low about 1 minute or 1–3 minutes by hand, until it's smooth and pillowy and holds soft peaks when the beater is lifted. If it starts to look coarse, styrofoamy, and overwhipped, just stir in a teaspoon of unbeaten cream to smooth it out again.

Acknowledgments

This book was a true labor of love, and many members of the community helped make it possible. First, my heartfelt thanks to my agent Amaryah Orenstein of GO Literary for championing this project and gracing my professional life with her enthusiasm and energy. I was delighted to work with Amy Lyons and the entire talented team at Globe Pequot knowing their long history of publishing books of regional interest. I'm thrilled with the result.

Thanks to my family for their support and good humor during this process, which involved turning the dining room into a photo studio and cramming the refrigerator, freezer, and all available kitchen surfaces full of baked goods, some highly questionable. Shout-outs to my teen sons: Nathaniel (chief chocolate consultant and brutal truthteller) and Max (for his super-taster skills and morale-boosting Spotify playlists). Special thanks to my husband, Rich, for washing untold numbers of dishes and putting up with my constant "talk to the hand" gestures.

Other folks I'd like to thank individually:

Carolyn, Bob, and Owen Manchek, my most called upon taste-testers, who have seen the frightening extremes of my baking habit and still live to tell the tale. And also for letting me raid their cabinets for ceramics, dishtowels, placemats, napkins, and random ingredients in a furious panic. The big bin of quilting fabric was the cherry on top.

Amy DiMatteo and Erin Jensen for recipe ideas, pandemic porch-based brainstorming, and tough love sessions. ("Turnip cake? That sounds disgusting.")

My sister, Trish Michael, who encouraged me to give this photography thing a try despite all evidence that it would be a complete disaster.

Eva Kosmas Flores and Bea Lubas, whose photography and food-styling classes made all the difference.

Hollis Schachner, for her beautiful handmade ceramics that grace many pages of this book.

Cathy Meyer for the old dog-chewed table that has become my favorite shooting surface.

Susanna Baird, Betsy Ellor, and the entire Carrot Cake writer's group in Salem for their support in all sorts of writing endeavors.

Erin Puranananda, Leslie Routman, Shona Simkin, and Juliet Harrison for their steadfast friendship over the years.

Sonia Pacheco for help with immigration research.

Tony Russo and the entire staff at the now former Russo's in Watertown, Massachusetts. There's a hole in my food-loving heart.

A huge thanks to my army of volunteer recipe-testers in New England and beyond (including a sizable Canadian contingent, one Aussie, and a gaggle of good-natured high school and middle school students). They include Amy Ayers; Carey A. Bates; Christine Bergsma; Katie Brossa; Adrienne Bruno; Katherine Candib; Don Chase; Tammy Schuetz Cook; Amy and Kristian DiMatteo; Kristen DiRocco; Katherine Elizabeth; Sarah Fitzpatrick; Nan Fornal; Tara R. Greco; Mimi Gross; Amy Viens Hutchinson; Sarah and Remy Jang; Erin and Jane Jensen; Kate Kendall and Dave and Claire Akeson; Karen Kirsten; Sandra Kogan; Michele Kosboth; Sarah and Simon Lewis; Jessica and Claire Mailman; Carolyn Manchek; Linda and Liam Manning; Maria May-Mardikis; Kristen and Peter Marriott; Cindy, Eliza, and Xander Martini; Rebecca Oja; Julie Peterson; Erin Puranananda; Jodi Riehl Ross; Amy Rothman; Hollis Schachner and Liat Stock; Rachel and Paige Seremeth; Shona Simkin; Marika St. Amand; Bronwen Tate; Erin and James Taylor; Lori and Mason Wiesner; Celeste Woodside; and Eileen Wozek.

Finally, I'd like to thank all the family and community-oriented farms and makers throughout New England. They include but are not limited to Carver Hill Orchard, Waltham Fields Community Farm, Drumlin Farm, Land's Sake Farm, Spring Brook Farm, Brigham Farm, Winter Moon Roots, Red Fire Farm, Codman Farm, and Chestnut Farms. Without them, we wouldn't eat nearly as well.

New England Resources

Find local farms, orchards, and farmers' markets

agriculture.nh.gov
guide.ctnofa.org
guide.farmfreshri.org
localharvest.org
mainefarmersmarkets.org
massfarmersmarkets.org
nofavt.org/find-organic-local-food

Coombs Family Farm, Brattleboro, VT
coombsfamilyfarms.com
Maple syrup, maple sugar

Formaggio Kitchen, Cambridge, MA
formaggiokitchen.com
Cheese, chocolate, baking supplies

Kimball Farm, Carlisle, MA; Lancaster, MA; Westford, MA; Jaffrey, NH
kimballfarm.com
Ice cream, honey, jam, maple syrup, maple sugar

King Arthur Flour, Norwich, VT
kingarthurbaking.com
Flour, malted milk powder, baking supplies, tools, pans

Labadie's Bakery, Lewiston, ME
labadiesbakery.com
Whoopie pies

Penzeys Spices, Arlington, MA; Hartford, CT; Norwalk, CT
penzeys.com
Spices, cocoa, vanilla, juniper berries

Wright's Dairy Farm & Bakery,
North Smithfield, RI
wrightsdairyfarm.com
Hermits, cakes, pies, cupcakes

Index

About the Author

Born in Maine, bred in New Hampshire, and a Massachusetts resident for more than 30 years, **Tammy Donroe Inman** is a New England writer, trained chef, and Boston-based cooking instructor. Her first book, *Wintersweet: Seasonal Desserts to Warm the Home*, has been praised by *USA Today*, the *Wall Street Journal*, the *Boston Globe*, *Edible Boston*, and *The Kitchn*. After earning her chops in the test kitchen of *Cook's Illustrated* magazine and the television show *America's Test Kitchen*, she spent nearly 20 years writing about food and developing recipes for *Fine Cooking*, *Parents*, *Yankee*, the *Boston Globe*, *Boston* magazine, *Cape Cod Life*, and *Serious Eats*. She taught hands-on cooking classes for adults and children at the Newton cooking school Create a Cook for 5 years. Inman has been interviewed by NPR's *All Things Considered*, *CBS Evening News*, and *The Atlantic* about her perspective on food. She was also the force behind the beloved blog *Food on the Food*. She lives outside of Boston with her husband, younger son (the eldest has flown the coop!), and two high-maintenance cats. To learn more, visit tammydonroe.com.